PICKING UP
THE
FLUTE

PICKING UP

THE

FLUTE

JOHN ELDER

GREEN WRITERS PRESS *Brattleboro, Vermont*

Printed in the United States

10 9 8 7 6 5 4 3 2 1

Green Writers Press is a Vermont-based publisher whose mission is to spread
a message of hope and renewal through the words and images we publish.
Throughout we will adhere to our commitment to preserving and protecting
the natural resources of the earth. To that end, a percentage of our proceeds
will be donated to environmental activist groups. Green Writers Press
gratefully acknowledges support from individual donors, friends, and readers
to help support the environment and our publishing initiative.

Giving Voice to Writers & Artists Who Will Make the World a Better Place
Green Writers Press | West Brattleboro, Vermont
www.greenwriterspress.com

Library of Congress Cataloging-in-Publication Data available upon request.
ISBN: 978-0-9961357-2-6

VISIT THE AUTHOR'S WEBSITE: WWW.JOHNELDERAUTHOR.COM

Flute icon photo by Sohier Christie
www.windwardflutes.com

PRINTED ON PAPER WITH PULP THAT COMES FROM FSC-CERTIFIED FORESTS, MANAGED FORESTS THAT
GUARANTEE RESPONSIBLE ENVIRONMENTAL, SOCIAL, AND ECONOMIC PRACTICES BY LIGHTNING
SOURCE ALL WOOD PRODUCT COMPONENTS USED IN BLACK & WHITE, STANDARD COLOR, OR SELECT
COLOR PAPERBACK BOOKS, UTILIZING EITHER CREAM OR WHITE BOOKBLOCK PAPER, THAT ARE
MANUFACTURED IN THE LAVERGNE, TENNESSEE PRODUCTION CENTER ARE
SUSTAINABLE FORESTRY INITIATIVE® (SFI®) CERTIFIED SOURCING

"This is that interval,
   that sweetest interval
      when love will blossom."

—William Carlos Williams
From the Coda to "Asphodel that Greeny Flower"

For Rita again

Contents

Prologue: *A Musical Interval*   *xi*

And Now for Something Completely Different
THE TRIP TO BIRMINGHAM   3

Hogback in Connemara
PLEASURES OF HOPE   27

Ecotones
LANGSTROM PONY   53

Lucky Old Man
JERRY'S BEAVER HAT, OR THE YANK'S RETURN   75

Shadows and Apples
THE MONTH OF JANUARY   101

Foregone Hillsides
ISLAND OF WOODS   133

Windings
THE PEACOCK'S FEATHER   157

The Smuggler's Path
O'CONNELL'S TRIP TO PARLIAMENT   183

Sky over the Common
THE BATTERING RAM AND LUCY FARR   199

Acknowledgments   223

Prologue:

A Musical Interval

∽

I NEVER EXPECTED TO DEVOTE so many hours each day to playing reels, jigs, hornpipes, polkas, barn dances, marches, flings, and slow airs on the wooden flute. But following my retirement from Middlebury College in June of 2010 this music became irresistible. Since my wife Rita (whose instrument is the concertina) often joined me in these traditional Irish tunes, they also became the hallmark of a new chapter in our marriage. On frosty evenings in the late fall and winter we would settle down in the living room for some music within the woodstove's envelope of comfort. As the weather warmed we moved out to the back deck and raised our melodies to the Hogback Ridge looming just to the east of our village of Bristol, Vermont. The light washing over that rocky slope of northern hardwoods modulated from gold to blue as we played together in the endless twilight of a New England summer. At dusk a skein of bats gusted out from under the loose slates roofing our house on North Street, flitting back and forth high above our heads. Favorite tunes like "My Darling Asleep" and "Banish Misfortune" flowed together into a soundtrack that lent wholeness to the shifting seasons of our life.

A couple of years before my retirement Rita had concluded her own career as a special educator at the elementary school in Lincoln—just a few miles farther up Mount Abraham from Bristol. Back when we were both still teaching, weekday mornings generally saw us driving off in different directions after a hurried breakfast. Now we could spend most days together in the rambling farmhouse where we had raised our children Rachel, Matthew, and Caleb. When we wanted some fresh air we would take walks with our Australian shepherd Shadowfax in the forested uplands surrounding Bristol. Such outings reminded us that we were living in the Green Mountains as well as in a big old house within a quaint village. Retirement thus became a *landscape* for us as well as a *time* in our lives. Our forays into the woods as well as our experience of marriage itself were in their turn permeated by all the tunes we struck up each day. These elements of our lives were, to borrow a term from Wordsworth, interfused.

⤷ A phrase from another poet I love has also helped me understand how retirement and music alike became the new terrain of marriage for Rita and me. *Mountain Interval* was the title Robert Frost gave to his third collection of poetry, published in 1916. It referred to the hanging valleys enfolded in New England's rugged ridges, so many of which harbor a compact village with its surrounding swirl of farms. Our own village is situated at the interval of Bristol Gap. A broad U, separating the main north-sound progression of the Green Mountains from its subsidiary Hogback Ridge, indicates where a glacier once slid through at this point. The surprisingly gentle shape of such glacial gaps is captured by an Irish word that I encountered in Tim Robinson's *Connemara* trilogy: *mám*, from the scooped-out summit of a pile of grain where a handful has been removed; from the curve of a breast. Both images evoke a place amid the flinty heights where the life of a family might be nurtured. Often, as at Bristol Gap, there is also a lower, V-shaped portion within the gap, marking the descent of a post-glacial stream. In our case this narrower valley within the wider, more ancient interval has been carved by the New Haven River intently pursuing its path west, until reaching Otter Creek then turning north with it to Lake Champlain.

Frost finds a second meaning in the phrase "mountain interval" too. Namely, as the period when we make ourselves at home in a particular landscape. In the years after Elinor and he were first married they lived on a series of farms so remote that they could feel as lonely and beautiful as a dream. Such isolated farmsteads always remained inextricable in their memories from these early episodes of their life together. Opening a first edition of the volume in question, a reader finds this dedication:

To You Who Least Need Reminding

that before this interval of the South Branch under black mountains, there was another interval, the Upper at Plymouth, where we walked in spring beyond the covered bridge; but that the first interval of all was the old farm, our brook interval, so called by the man we had it from in sale

The musical interval described in this memoir lasted for almost four years, from my retirement until the moment when we suddenly needed to change our plans again. Just as we had not anticipated the importance that Irish music would assume in our lives, we also did not foresee that we would suddenly need to sell our family home in order to build a smaller, more accessible house. But Rita was diagnosed with a neurological condition that will eventually decrease her mobility, and we decided it was better to make a change sooner rather than later. This meant that much of 2014 was dominated by selling our old house, having a smaller one built, and getting rid of most of our furniture and books. The fact that a couple with a three-year-old son bought our North Street home the week after we put it on the market also meant that we were living out of suitcases in houses and apartments made available by generous friends during the five months before February of 2015 arrived and we were finally able to settle into our own new place at 19 Mountain Street in Bristol. That's the address where I'm now writing the prologue for a book that was largely produced in the study of our previous house on North Street.

I look at this four-year period of being utterly entranced by Irish music as a distinct chapter in our lives because its end, as well as its beginning, turned out to be so clearly defined. Though we've returned gratefully to our daily sharing of tunes, after the past year in which the demands of a move disrupted both our musical practice and our pace of learning new pieces, the fact of the matter is that Ireland's traditional music has now gone from being a primary context of our life to being one lovely element in it. Even as the intensity of the earlier interval recedes, though, it remains for us, as Virginia Woolf says, "one of those globed compacted things over which thought lingers and love plays." It is a landmark in the topography of our marriage.

In his essay "The Figure a Poem Makes," Frost wrote, "No surprise for the writer, no surprise for the reader." What at first felt to me like a musical spree gradually grew into much more. One big surprise has been how often I turn to the same cluster of *writers* when trying to express what playing Irish tunes on the flute has meant to me. Wordsworth, Frost, and Woolf have already been mentioned. In the chapters that follow I also refer to the Twenty-Third Psalm of David, Virgil's first Eclogue, and a remarkable essay by Leslie Marmon Silko. These are all works that powerfully shaped my teaching for many years. Tim Robinson, the chronicler and cartographer of Connemara, has become similarly important to me for his deep insights into the meaning of the Irish landscape. But in touching on such writers my intention is never critical analysis. The simple fact is that these are works I love, and that are are naturally linked for me with other beloved people and things.

My whole adult life has revolved around literature. Had I made my living as a rancher, a politician, or a doctor, old experiences of cattle and rangeland, contested elections, or difficult diagnoses might now help me to convey the direction and shape of new endeavors. At the same time, I want to declare that the poetry and nature writing instead coming to mind for me, as a recently retired professor, are much more than convenient comparisons. I believe that literature is, as D. H. Lawrence called it, "the Bright Book of Life." Bringing such formative works into the narrative is essential to locating both these explorations of Ireland's traditional music and my retirement from Middlebury College within the larger landscape of my experience. It is like referring to the rugged Hogback Ridge behind our village when I want to convey my sense of home, like recalling exchanges with my parents many years ago that can still foster my capacity for hope today, like playing the flute to Rita's concertina as we venture into the shifting terrain of our life together.

In the same way that books have oriented me on the path from full-time teaching to a passion for Irish music, so too a specific sequence of tunes has guided me along the way. Such tunes, learned by ear and often memorized by endless repetition within a period of just a week or two, become firmly linked with particular moments in a player's life. Ten tunes accordingly map my progression through the chapters of this memoir. Because *Picking Up the Flute* is the record of my own challenges, fascinations, and reflections as a late-life beginner, I decided to record those nine tunes myself rather than using tracks from CDs by leading Irish musicians. I've come only so far—as one may hear. Still, playing the wooden flute has already bestowed the gift of much deeper appreciation for this rich tradition's beauty. My intention in these recorded renditions is to share the grateful discoveries of one ardent amateur.

↩ On a wooden, or "simple-system," flute the six finger holes are open, rather than being covered with the cunning, inter-locked lids of a modern silver instrument. The holes vary in diameter but are all considerably larger than those, say, of a soprano recorder. In fingering the notes of a tune one's soft fingertips thus press firmly down into those sharply incised circles. After first taking the flute out of its case each day my hands are especially alert to the vibrating passage of air just below those holes. When I finally put the flute back down again I find dark red circles imprinted in the first three fingers of each hand. After practicing in the morning I carry these fading mementos in my flesh as I turn to other projects. Lying in the silent darkness beside Rita after we have been playing in the evening I can register my pulse in fingertips still awakened by music. Through writing *Picking Up the Flute* I have come to understand how inextricable marriage and memory, illness and healing are for me from the haunting beauty of Irish music. As one chapter in our musical life draws to a close, the tunes Rita and I continue to play together offer us a resource on which to draw in affirming whatever comes next.

A NOTE TO THE READER

When you see this flute icon, click to the link for the author's website at **www.johnelderauthor.com** *to listen to the example or song being featured then in this interactive book.*

And Now for Something Completely Different

THE TRIP TO BIRMINGHAM

I MARVEL, EACH SPRING AND EARLY SUMMER, at the flocks of warblers yawing across the backyards of our Vermont village. Suddenly, and at top speed, they turn together as if directed by a single mind. Half a dozen years ago Rita and I discovered that a long-wed couple too could veer, and veer again, in unison. We both loved our teaching jobs, hers in special education at Lincoln School, mine in English and Environmental Studies at Middlebury College. But when she decided in 2008 to retire after twenty-five satisfying years of supporting families and coaching kids who had a hard time reading, I suddenly began to consider retirement too.

It had been such a privilege to teach Middlebury's terrific students and also to collaborate with colleagues from a wide range of disciplines. Rita's choice nonetheless made me think about drawing a line in my life and finding out what might be on the other side. For one thing, now that our three children were launched in their adult lives and she herself would be less professionally occupied, I wanted to make the most of this opportunity to hang out together. As June of 2010 approached, however, and with it the date I had arranged for my retirement, I confided to her that I was feeling quite a pang about leaving the college where I had spent my entire teaching career. Rita's response was as liberating as it was unexpected: "Whether you retire now or in five years, of course you'll feel a pang. The only question is, when do you want it?" Without hesitation I said, "I'll take my pang now!"

In this mood of freedom and spontaneity we ended up making an even more surprising decision, perhaps in part as a playful way to set the seal on our retirement. We had been devoted amateur musicians for most of our lives, with Rita playing the piano and me the French horn. At the end of our high school years in different California towns we had each seriously considered attending a conservatory. Instead we both decided to enroll at Pomona College, where we met in the choir during my senior year. We married following Rita's graduation in 1970, moved to Connecticut where she earned her Master's in Special Education and I finished up a doctorate in English at Yale, found teaching jobs in Vermont's Champlain Valley, and raised our three children here. Even in the midst of our absorbing vocations and family life, we managed to continue playing chamber music with friends in the college community. Performances of Brahms's Trio for Horn, Piano, and Violin and of Poulenc's Sextet for Piano and Wind Quintet were among the highlights for us.

In the summer of 2008, however, a season bookended by Rita's recent retirement and my impending one, we decided on a whim both to change instruments and to pursue a different musical tradition. I can't remember now which of us came up with the bright idea of concentrating on traditional Irish music, but we flung ourselves into the new project with glee. The astonishment of our musical friends made it seem the joke of a lifetime. For Rita this meant taking up that devilish little contraption the Anglo concertina, on which the same button produces different notes when pressing the bellows together and drawing it out again. She bought a Morse concertina at a musical emporium in western Massachusetts called the Button Box. Meanwhile I went online to order a keyless wooden flute in D. We both quickly became devoted to Ireland's musical landscape with its shadowed, modal melodies and jaunty rhythms. From the beginning, playing this quirky dance-music put me into a trance. The tunes unspooled in my mind throughout the day, while the ones Rita and I played together after supper echoed through my dreams as well.

This would be the moment to specify, though, that *Picking Up the Flute* is the story of my own journey into these Irish tunes and not hers. Her book would need to be called *Picking Up the Concertina* for one thing. In addition, the meaning of this melodic interlude has turned out to be inseparable for me not only from our marriage but also from my reading and teaching over almost four decades at Middlebury. Beyond being simply a light-hearted diversion, and a refreshing contrast to the previous projects of my professional life, it has become a lens. In the same way that marriage and retirement were the context for my learning to play the Irish flute, the musical tradition which I have entered with this instrument in hand has broadened my view of both the pastoral literature on which my teaching focused and the reforested Vermont ridge beside which we live.

The unanticipated dialogue between my new musical practice and the books so close to my heart has been deepened by their common roots in suffering. Ireland's defiant music flows from a history of suppression and starvation, just as the pastoral ideal originally awoke in landscapes and communities broken by imperial violence. My hope to enter retirement at a dancing tempo has been challenged by the persistence of such connections, as well as by the serious illness that turned out to be waiting for Rita on the far side of sixty-five. Down we have dived into the currents of this music, sometimes playing for three or four hours a day, as if seeking the healing spell promised by the title of a tune like "Banish Misfortune." Toward the end of the interval described in this book, playing the flute sometimes felt to me like wrestling lamely with an angel. But it has not withheld its blessing. That's the story I can tell.

⌐ In the summer of 2009, we attended the Catskills Irish Arts Week in East Durham, New York for the first time. I signed up for an intermediate-level workshop in the Irish flute with Catherine McEvoy, a celebrated performer and teacher in the Roscommon tradition. Registering in her intermediate class was certainly a stretch for me, since in the months after acquiring my flute I'd only had a couple of introductory lessons. My main exposure thus far to this musical tradition had come from buying several books and starting to play a selection of the traditional tunes printed in them. Though traveling to the Catskills expressed my commitment to taking the next steps with the flute, I was clueless about how much of the workshop's challenge for me would in fact come down to learning and memorizing tunes by ear.

Trying to learn Irish music in this traditional way sometimes made me feel as if, body and mind, I was in a vise. The only experience I could compare it with was the fight-or-flight intensity of studying Japanese at Middlebury College long after I had joined the faculty there. Catherine McEvoy, like my earlier Japanese instructors Mutsuko Endo Simon and Nobuo Ogawa, was gracious and calm but also highly exacting. Though she definitely had my full attention, I wasn't at all sure that I would be up to the challenge. Just as whole sentences from our Japanese drills throbbed in my head after hours of concentrating in class, so too did the musical segments Catherine played for us—first to memorize separately and then to string together into an entire tune.

One of my chief resources in sticking with Japanese had been a remark my admired Middlebury colleague John Berninghausen made to me at the college gym in the summer before my first semester of this new language. "Your brain is too old to learn Japanese," he remarked bluntly, on the basis of his experience as a seasoned professor of Chinese—fighting words that I repeated truculently to myself as we quickly began to rely almost exclusively on Japanese during class and then as I needed to devote longer and longer evenings to the dialogues we were asked to memorize. Though I did manage to keep up with my eighteen-year-old comrades in the course, my brain was in fact stretched to the utmost by the task of taking in a new language by ear and then formulating my own sentences that incorporated our new idioms and constructions.

When I took up the Irish flute I was twenty years older than when I started Japanese in the lead-up to a sabbatical in Kyoto. Taking in tunes by ear and retaining them for the next day's class thus stimulated even more adrenaline and terror in me than those language drills had. Though invariably polite and friendly, Catherine turned her gaze toward us with an air of honed attentiveness when it was time for my colleagues and me to stand and deliver. It felt like coming face-to-face with one of the Fates.

Students in our Japanese class were asked to learn and absorb dialogues before we had sufficient background to grasp them fully. We had no recourse other than to hang in there uncertainly and work by inference. But with the help of the teachers' miming and repetition we figured out, for example, that "*Ima nanji desu ka*" meant "What time is it?" (The answer in the corresponding weekly dialogue was eternally "*Shichiji desu,*" "It's seven o'clock," though in the follow-up drills we got to exercise a small measure of creativity by making it "*goji,*" "*rokuji,*" and other hours of our choosing.) A similar progression from confusion to consolidation occurred during the process of memorizing my favorite piece from Catherine's workshop, a reel by the flute-player and composer Josie McDermott called "The Trip to Birmingham." After learning it in class and then sweating over it for hours on a bench across the road from Gavin's (the old-fashioned hotel where we stayed along with many other participants in the Irish Arts Week) I finally found the fragmented phrases coalescing into an intoxicating tune. I could feel its exhilarating momentum, count it to myself in one, and delight in its upward and downward swoops. This tune remains a musical landmark for me, even after years in which Rita and I have learned hundreds of other pieces together.

↫ Much of the ornamentation characteristic of Irish music can be related to the sound of the bagpipes in Celtic traditions. Because most pipes rely on a continuous stream of air, the notes need to be separated and the phrases shaped by such techniques as a tap on the tone immediately below the main note or a quick cut on the one immediately above it. If a G were the main note a tap would be accomplished on the flute by briefly touching the F# hole, right below the covered G, with the index finger of the right hand. For a cut the hole for the A just above that G would be quickly uncovered and then closed again by the middle finger of the left hand. Notice that the main effect of both actions is to emphasize the G itself. Another common ornament on Irish instruments is the roll, which rapidly repeats three eighth notes by inserting first a cut and then a tap. Performers on the fiddle and concertina continue to use all of these elements even though they could easily separate notes in other ways with their fingers or bow, while flute players also do so even though we could simply employ tonguing with our mouth-blown instruments. Such ways of articulating are essential to the distinctive quality of

LINK:
Examples of a Cut, a Tap, and a Roll

9

Irish music, lending energy to simple tunes, and enriching the timbre of sessions in which mixed-instrument groups play the same sequence of melodies together.

The key is to execute the ornamentation with such briskness that the basic notes sound strongly while the articulations swiftly slip in and out, more felt than heard. Entering into Catherine McEvoy's workshop I knew in a theoretical sense how to play these various ornaments, but because I lacked the requisite deftness, there remained a doggedness in my phrasing that contrasted unhappily to the grace and bounce achieved by more expert players. In addition to being a sprightly and delightful tune, because of its profusion of rolls "The Trip to Birmingham" also felt like a timely clinic in this form of ornamentation. In practicing rolls before, I had steeled myself, taken a breath, and launched forth in trepidation. In the "Trip to Birmingham" the rolls never stopped coming, so there was really no choice but to flow along with them.

LINK: *The Trip to Birmingham*

↬ It's hard to reach any firm conclusions about Irish tunes from their titles, which can be whimsical to the extreme. One obvious aspect of the name "The Trip to Birmingham," though, is that it's related to a specific place. Many other titles, like "The Trip to Athlone" and "The Humours of Ballymote," further exemplify how often tunes and towns are linked in some way for the musicians who composed them. In class Catherine gave us a bit more background about the title of this particular reel. It originated in the context of a musical tour across England by Josie McDermott, a celebrated blind Irish flute player who was also a friend of their family when she was growing up in Birmingham. Arrangements for the composer to travel to that city by train broke down and a last-minute drive became necessary. The reel, like the trip, rolls down the road with high spirits just one step shy of frantic. The piece's energy and hilarity are heightened in the tune's second part, which opens an octave above the G of the piece's opening section, substitutes a full-fledged roll for the earlier section's initial cut, and then trumps that high G roll with yet another roll on high A.

We eight participants in the Catskills workshop played "The Trip to Birmingham" over and over for most of one hour-and-a-half morning meeting, after which we listened to it on our various little digital recorders at spare moments in the afternoon and evening—hoping to solidify this tune in our memory before being presented with a half-dozen other pieces over the course of a week. At the end of that week, Catherine McEvoy gave each of us "the ABCs" of all the pieces we had just learned so that we could continue to consult them in that form. Here's what her transcription of "Trip to Birmingham" looked like in this format favored by many traditional musicians.

↪ With the exceptions of a plus sign, indicating a pause of one beat, or a dash, which means that the final note of a line is elongated, all letters stand for eighth notes within the conventional cut-time of a reel. A little "1" at the upper right of a letter shows that it's one octave up from the lower end of the flute's register, while an underlined and elevated "R" is the symbol for a roll. A highly accomplished Irish musician like Catherine McEvoy will of course vary her ornamentation and other forms of interpretation from one performance of a tune to the next. But this hand-written version still gave us students a highly useful aid to memory for the basic tune as we continued to solidify what we had learned after the Catskills workshop was over.

One explanation for such a method of transcription is that some traditional Irish musicians mastered their instruments by ear in childhood and never bothered, or had the opportunity, to learn standard musical notation. Even for the many Irish performers today who are thoroughly at home with conventional sheet music, though, there remains a special value in this more idiosyncratic method for writing out tunes. For one thing, it symbolizes the primacy of ear over eye in their tradition. ABCs are merely prompts for tunes already residing in a player's ear, mind, and muscle memory. Traditional musicians' often unenthusiastic attitude toward sheet music is suggested in the delightfully dismissive term they use for it: "the dots." What a paltry affair those dots are, that choice of words implies, in comparison to the sustained focus represented by memorization—as well as to the relationship with the teacher, performer, or fellow player from whom one has received a particular tune. I have been struck by traditional Irish musicians' carefulness about crediting the person from whom they received, or "got," certain tunes. It reminds me of a similar punctiliousness when traditional storytellers, both in Native American and Appalachian contexts, acknowledge the specific lineage of tales they now bring to new listeners.

The ABC system has been strangely liberating for me, as a musician who played from sheet music for over fifty years. When I look at a tune in that more familiar format I can immediately hear both the pitches and the rhythms. Perhaps my relationship with ABCs would be similar if I had been accustomed to this approach for that long. But for now at least when I first glance back at Catherine McEvoy's written rendering of "The Trip to Birmingham" it's pretty opaque for me both rhythmically and tonally until I have worked out the first couple of measures. Then the whole, previously memorized piece comes flooding back and I don't have to consult the written record further unless I find myself stumbling at some later point.

This minimalist, jerry-rigged, yet also practical way of transcribing tunes evokes generations of performers making do with what they had. And in this regard the history and evolution of the musical tradition are of course inseparable from Irish history as a whole. The poverty of colonized Ireland meant that when concertinas lost their popularity in nineteenth-century England the Irish could afford to incorporate these cast-off instruments into their own musical expression.

Similarly, when silver Boehm flutes replaced six-keyed wooden ones in the orchestras of Europe the old wooden flutes were shipped to Ireland in barrels and sold there for pennies. Some Irish musicians took off the keys and corked the holes where they had been attached so that the flutes could now be fingered exactly like pennywhistles, while others preferred to mess around with the keys. When the 1840s came, and with it the Great Hunger, many thousands of Irish immigrants arrived in America, occasionally managing to include instruments in their scanty stowage but more often simply transporting tunes in their minds and fingers. Transplanted players established cities like New York, Chicago, Pittsburgh, and St. Louis as centers of Irish music to this day.

The life of teaching, studying, advising students, and writing that absorbed me at Middlebury College changed—especially after my exposure in the Catskills to a world-class Irish musician like Catherine McEvoy—into one dominated by listening, practicing, and taking music lessons. It was almost as if I had ended up going to conservatory after all. Except, of course, that there were no books of études, that I was not playing in an orchestra, and that I couldn't manage to find a regular teacher of the Irish flute in our part of Vermont. Lessons now were catch-as-catch-can and sometimes needed to focus on correcting errors I'd fallen into while trying to teach myself. None of these limitations ever dampened my excitement about the music, though. In this regard the story of my flute playing seems to parallel the experience of many other Baby Boomers, fortunate enough to afford retirement, who have in fact made that choice. By contrast with earlier American cohorts, ours often seems inclined to approach this transition not as an opportunity to rest after our careers but instead as a portal into adventures and discoveries—even as an opportunity to forge new identities.

Such expectations can of course be a fantasy or, as Freud would say, an illusion—something we anticipate wishfully rather than because of the evidence. My fingers won't ever again move as fast as a fifteen-year-old's, I don't have the wind I had as a young horn player, and the tunes I memorize with such effort tend to slip back out of my mind. Still, it's been a deep satisfaction persevering, and achieving incremental gains, as a flute player. Little by little, Rita and I also build up the list of tunes we possess together, while particular pieces we've already known for several years will suddenly blossom anew for us. The rhythmic arcs lengthen and the mind of a tune, the heart of a tune, is disclosed. Though my musical capacities are in certain ways diminished by age and by starting over on a new instrument, my love of music has never been greater. I have found that the meaning of retirement often resides in this combination of holding on and opening up.

Musical technique begins, of course, with careful listening. In this regard, Catherine McEvoy was determined to help us hear the way in which every eighth note in a jig's groupings of three has its own, entirely distinct weight and velocity. The dominance of the initial note in a threesome, followed by the lightness and brevity of the second one and the intermediate heft of the third, lend a lovely flowing quality to a jig like "Maid on the Green." Here's how that tune begins. Such a way of shaping the rhythm, when played by a masterful performer like Catherine or the late, lamented Mike Rafferty, can promote a sense of headlong excitement in the music that is at the same time balanced by a calm, unrushed feeling.

LINK: *Maid on the Green*

Such technical and interpretive subtleties sometimes continue to feel quite challenging for me, especially by contrast with the confidence I had developed in a different idiom while playing the French horn. But by the same token it has enlarged the world in which I (and my fingers) move. Though I never have found a regular flute teacher in Vermont I have been lucky enough to enroll in the workshops on Irish repertoire taught in Montpelier and Waterbury every fall and spring by the piper Benedict Koehler and the button-accordion player Hilari Farrington. Benedict and Hilari also put me in touch with Brad Hurley, an outstanding flute player and teacher with whom it's been possible to arrange for occasional lessons at his home in Montréal, at ours in Bristol, as well as over Skype.

Catherine McEvoy and these other three skilled teachers all exemplify the special qualities of tact, sympathy, and alertness to developmental stages required to teach adult learners effectively. They bear in mind their older students' combination of considerable experience in kindred fields and strong motivation on the one hand with rudimentary skills and a certain physical creakiness. As Benedict remarked to our group one evening in Montpelier, "If you take up this music as an adult you can be good or you can be fast but you can't always be both at the same time!" I found this comment both accurate and encouraging in the same way as Rita's statement about retirement's inevitable pang. My goal, then, is to be good, which is to say musical, even as I try to keep my footing amid the whirl of reels and jigs. Also, cheerful in encountering my own limitations.

⌒ A certain comical cluelessness, which has often characterized my approach as a late-life beginner on the Irish flute, is linked for me with a humorous encounter in Connemara, just as my interest in playing the Irish flute was really taking off. I was invited to Ireland for a week of conversation among writers who shared my own focus on landscape. This informal symposium took place at the home of Máiréad and Tim Robinson in the picturesque village of Roundstone. I was especially happy to participate in this group convened by the Robinsons and the writer Leslie Van Gelder because I had already begun to read Tim's books about the Aran Islands and Connemara with the greatest admiration. The dozen other writers in attendance, who came from Canada, the United States, New Zealand, and England as well as from Ireland, formed a particularly congenial and stimulating group.

Still, it was a welcome break, on a brisk spring afternoon, to slip into a quiet harborside pub for a late lunch on my own. I ordered an open-faced sandwich with crab from the local waters, and a tall glass of cider. The pubkeeper, his bar well wiped and his last glass polished, seemed to feel time weighing heavily in his otherwise empty establishment. Soon enough he hove up to my table by the window with a look of bland friendliness.

"So was it wanting to see where your old folks came from that brought you to Connemara then?" His orotund, performative brogue hinted that he was hoping to pass a pleasant hour by amiably mocking the latest in an endless series of Irish-American tourists.

If I had offered anything at all to work with in terms of local family associations he would have been off and running. To the mention of a great-grandfather's farm near Clifden, for instance, I could hear him exclaiming, "And don't I know just the place!" But his apparent readiness for some such harmless foolery found no purchase in my own lineage. When I said, "You know, I actually don't have a drop of Irish blood," his voice jumped up an octave and he asked, seemingly with as much pleasure as disappointment at this shift from a familiar scenario, "Really?" He sat down with me then for a less scripted conversation about my family's home in Vermont and what each of us perceived to be its intriguing similarities to his in Connemara.

This memorable encounter in the Roundstone pub continues to reverberate with the unexpected centrality of traditional Irish music in my life following retirement from Middlebury College. The tunes swirling through my head seemed to have little to do with either my familial heritage or my concerns as a teacher of English and Environmental Studies over the better part of four decades. I took them to represent a more light-hearted impulse—a holiday from long-established obligations, as symbolized by the clock one of our sons and his wife gave me upon retirement that had all the numbers jumbled at the bottom of the dial and "Whatever!" written across its center. Still, as that jocular pub-keeper had understood from the start, even when we're in a festive mood there's often some back-story ticking insistently against our new days off the clock. Just as emigration from one's homeland is a stark fact never quite erased by assimilation and success in a new country, so too retirement can never bring a complete release from the intense commitments that preceded it for so many years. Ireland and its music have not replaced the reading, ideas, and relationships of my life as a teacher and householder. They have syncopated them, though, like the rolling sway that propels a jig or makes a reel into a hornpipe.

⏎ Retiring from Middlebury had felt like an occasion for grieving as well as celebration. When the evening arrived for me to address the Middlebury College community for one last time, I couldn't stop thinking about Mrs. Ramsay in *To the Lighthouse*. For me, the section of Virginia Woolf's novel called "The Dinner Party" summed up the alchemy that can occur in a classroom. A collection of distracted or timid individuals can suddenly fuse into a vivid community, just as Mrs. Ramsay's previously self-absorbed guests all at once became aware of participating in a remarkable occasion as they gathered around that table in a ramshackle summer house. This transformation in the novel happened immediately after she, nearly in despair, had called out "Light the candles." "Now all the candles were lit up, and the faces on both sides of the table were brought nearer by the candlelight and composed, as they had not been in the twilight, into a party round a table . . . Some change at once went through them all, as if this had really happened, and they were all conscious of making a party together in a hollow, on an island; had their common cause against that fluidity out there."

Such coalescence can't, of course, be achieved in every meeting of a seminar—or at every dinner party. On days when I returned home disappointed by the level of conversation in a class, I'm afraid I tended to act more like that egomaniacal academic *Mr.* Ramsay, who morosely muttered lines like "We perish each alone" as he trawled shamelessly for sympathy from his over-burdened wife. Still, there were always more than enough of what Virginia Woolf calls "moments of being" to keep me going as a teacher. And now, looking back at my long history in this superb liberal arts college, my heart was filled by the memory of such experiences.

In standing up to give my farewell lecture on the evening of April 22, 2010, though, I was identifying specifically with Mrs. Ramsay when the moment came for her to *leave* the dinner party. It was time for me too to relinquish a beloved conversation. As she departed from the gathering into which so much of her creative effort had flowed, Mrs. Ramsay paused at the door of the dining room to look back for one last time: "It was necessary now to carry everything a step further. With her foot on the threshold she waited a moment longer in a scene which was vanishing even as she looked, and then, as she moved and took Minta's arm and left the room, it changed, it shaped itself differently; it had become, she knew, giving one last look at it over her shoulder, already the past."

My own elegiac hesitation at the moment of retirement did not come from a tendency to idealize the college community. Heated battles over curriculum can arise in any institution, and they certainly did from time to time at Middlebury. Over the years, I came to feel that such conflicts generally had less to do with the ostensible terms of opposition than with the interplay between two different impulses that can lead people into academic work. The first is the love of continually learning new things; the second a desire to cultivate and deepen expertise. While most professors will have a mixture of these impulses, one or the other is often predominant. This contrast is yet another manifestation of the rough tug-of-war between romantic and classical visions that has organized Western culture for the last two and a half centuries. Emotion and discovery versus order and clarity.

While I appreciate the importance of both modes, the romantic has always been to the fore in my temperament. The founding Abbott of the San Francisco Zen Center, Shunryu Suzuki, wrote, "In the beginner's mind there are many possibilities, but in the expert's mind there are few." For me, after a career of teaching new courses whenever possible, shifting from an appointment in English to a split-position in English and Environmental Studies, and concluding as a non-departmental College Professor with a special interest in service-learning courses, retirement felt like another grand opportunity to seek beginner's mind. I would step back from the groomed campus of Middlebury College to the shaggy third-growth forest of the Hogback Ridge rising behind our home in the village of Bristol. I would turn in my tweed jacket and briefcase for the jeans, flannel shirts, and hiking boots of my youth in the Bay Area, and then I would see what happened.

Given such a temperament, it's perhaps not surprising that a new enthusiasm should have soon swept me away like a latter-day Mr. Toad. The word obsession might almost be suggested by the swarm of related activities buzzing into my days as I started to learn the flute. In fact, though, such intense engagement with Irish music has never felt compulsive or burdensome to me. It has instead offered an experience of renewal—an absorbing adventure that has at the same time deepened my sense of affiliation with our home landscape, illuminated the pastoral literature that had been at the heart of my teaching, and lent its own vividness to marriage with Rita in our fifth decade together.

It's certainly not that retirement has been altogether idyllic either. Just as Rita and I have both faced challenges to our health, we have also been saddened by the struggles of people we love. Our Bristol community too has faced polarizing controversies about its future, while looming over the beautiful circle of the seasons here has been the specter of climate change. Even in the face of these difficulties and concerns, however, picking up the flute has turned out to be a vehicle for freshness in each day. It has helped me to inhabit the present rather than being drawn too much into anxiety or regret.

A rhythm of divergence and return has proven to be my organizing principle in this book. In turning to Irish music I have stepped away from my earlier vocation and identity. But again and again, prompted by some aspect of a tune, I have also found myself swept back into a lifetime's images and associations. Such reflections can sometimes form a bridge between two tunes. When that happens I can tap my foot again to mark the downbeat of the next musical figure and keep playing. In teaching, writing, travel, and family, just as in many a tune, apparent departures can circle back home, achieving their integration and fulfillment just when they seemed to be gone forever. Such a process of rounding off resembles the moment in an Irish session when the player who has initiated a set looks up into the eyes of other musicians in the circle to signal that this will be the last time through.

I have felt stirred by the degree to which this musical path has also enriched my sense of Vermont. One reason its tunes have transformed my outlook is that they have swept Ireland so briskly into my frame of reference. Our family has no Irish heritage, as I have said, though my mother's forebears did camp out in Ulster for a couple of centuries en route from the Lowlands to Appalachia. And despite loving the writing of Yeats, Joyce, and Heaney for many years I had never really known much about their country. As Rita and I began traveling to County Clare and County Galway for their music, however, I got hooked by their landscapes and history too. Similarly, through reading and meeting Tim Robinson I came to recognize certain intriguing geological and historical parallels between his Connemara and our family's home in Vermont.

For one thing, following the path of Irish music into a deeper acquaintance with Connemara has reinforced the fact that the densely forested landscape of Vermont is as much an artifact of loss and suffering as western Ireland's windswept hills. It has confirmed that the pastoral literature on which my teaching focused for so long is only valid when it explicitly returns to the vexed history from which it grew. Such associations have served to make playing the flute back home in the Green Mountains not only a daily musical practice but also a context for attempting to live more concretely in place. The tunes that emerged from Ireland's long travail and that still reverberate in its haunted beauty now take root in my own life and landscape. I feel them in my fingers as I climb the ragged, third-growth slope that rises above our village. Hearing their echoes now, I can open my heart to the consolation within their spirit of resistance.

Flute playing has thus felt to me like both a youthful spree and its opposite. It has proven to be at once the start of something entirely different and an opportunity for delving more deeply into the content and meaning of the books that have been important to me for so long. In that final talk at Middlebury I had expected to be stepping over a threshold, with everything I'd known and done as a teacher "becoming already the past." Instead I have found my foot still suspended above it, arrested by a conversation still audible from a room I assumed had already been left behind. As I now continue, like Mrs. Ramsay, to look back over my shoulder, my main feeling is one of surprise that, even in the act of stepping away, I remain right here.

Hogback in Connemara

THE PLEASURES OF HOPE

Rain is general all over Connemara. In every month
of the year and for parts, at least, of two days out of three, it
swirls in over Roundstone Bog then drums down onto Errisbeg,
the highest point within that marshy sprawl. Some of these
spatters will wash due south, over the two-lobed peninsula
of Goirtín and out to sea, without relying on a fixed channel.
Others, relinquishing their individual surface tension after
being hung up in the sphagnum, will pool eastward over the
sheep tracks that edge the bog, eventually arriving at the newly
paved roads and driveways of an uninhabited housing estate.
Now they can hasten toward Roundstone Bay, running past the
dockside studio of Folding Landscapes where Tim and Máiréad
Robinson produce their remarkable maps and gazetteers. But
the drops trickling north and east from Errisbeg will gather
into rivulets that trace a network of softly inscribed glens.
These will become the tributaries for dozens of irregular lochs

strewn across the bog's interior like puzzle pieces scattered on a table. Visible streams connect some of these bodies of water to one another, while arteries under the peat link the whole system into one soggy pulsation.

While growing ever more interested in Ireland through playing the flute I also became absorbed in the work of Tim Robinson and the landscape surrounding his and Máiréad's home in Roundstone. His compelling books about the Aran Islands and Connemara, along with their extraordinarily precise maps of those locales and the nearby region known as the Burren, grounded my appreciation for Irish music firmly in Counties Clare and Galway. The years 2010 through 2014, in addition to ushering in my retirement and Rita's and my musical spree, included several celebrations of Robinson's achievements, which I was invited to attend in Roundstone, Galway, and Dublin.

On three such occasions I traveled to Ireland on my own, while on two others Rita was able to join me. The musicians, writers, and naturalists we met in Connemara and Galway during this period have become a valued community for us. So too certain paths and vistas to which I found myself returning again and again, like those within Roundstone Bog, have become important points of reference. The intriguing new constellation of friendship, literature, and topography on both sides of the Atlantic Ocean complemented the infatuation Rita and I were experiencing with Irish music. The tunes we were playing every day and the retirement on which we had both embarked unfolded within an ever-broadening circle of watersheds.

"Catchment" is the word Tim Robinson prefers for designating a unit of the earth's surface, bounded by higher edges, within which springs, rainfall, and smaller tributaries all converge before flowing on into some broader system of drainages. Every point on the earth's surface is mapped in such a way by elevation and the movement of water. In *Listening to the Wind*, the first volume of his *Connemara* trilogy, Robinson further characterizes a catchment as "an open, self-renewing system, supporting and supported by a vast number of life-forms and all their interrelations. Even its basic topography, the most skeletal and reductive representation of its geometry, is profoundly suggestive of a way of looking at the world and caring for it." As Gary Snyder has pointed out, our entire planet and its oceans must ultimately be considered as a single, unified catchment.

"Watershed" is the word we more commonly use in the United States for what Robinson calls a catchment. David Brynn, a neighbor who has founded an organization called Vermont Family Forests, applies this concept of confluence within a clearly defined topography to many aspects of our community and economy. The firewood we harvest sustainably and on which many of us in Bristol rely for heating our homes comes, for David, from the five-town "woodshed" or "heatshed" of northeastern Addison County. He calls the writing produced here, and the literature studied in our new neighbors-teaching-neighbors initiative, Hogback Community College, our "bookshed." It's not that we read *only* books from this watershed, or course, though both the poetry of Frost and our region's original Abenaki stories do take on a special meaning here. The point is, though, that tracing any element of our culture and livelihood back to its source inevitably brings one local map edge to edge with others. The pursuit of traditional Irish music has in this way made me want to know more about Ireland's landscape. Conversely, my sense of affiliation with the Green Mountains looming above our home prepared me both to love that music and to experience our landscape's kinship with heights known as the Nine Pins that preside over Roundstone Bog.

Highly localized writing, music, and art anywhere in the world hold great importance for the inhabitants of other rural areas striving to discern and to convey the significance of their own home-landscapes. In his books and maps, Robinson perpetuates a tradition of Romantic revolt against centralized, mechanized, and hierarchical views of humanity and the land. In an essay from *The Spirit of the Age*, William Hazlitt identified the genius of Wordsworth's early poetry as "a proud humility," taking "the commonest events and objects, as a test to prove that nature is always interesting from its inherent truth and beauty . . ." In the rapt attention Robinson brings to "the thousands of tiny trickles" in a catchment, he also asserts the significance of a boggy region located far from any capital, as well as at the extreme western edge not only of Ireland but also of Europe.

As a fellow denizen of the hinterlands, though living far from Ireland, I feel personally grateful for Tim Robinson's example of dogged and eccentric excellence at this ancient edge. By focusing on what Snyder would call the lineaments of the land, rather than on political boundaries, Robinson invites his readers to enter into a collective effort of re-mapping and re-storying our homes on earth. My own point of access into this collaborative project has turned out to be through a *dialogue* between the Roundstone Bog—both as I have experienced it on foot and as it is depicted in Robinson's writing and maps—and the history and terrain of our neighboring Hogback Ridge. Such connections are more than intriguing parallels. They are also a principal context within which I can reflect on both Irish music and the chapter of Rita's and my marriage that began in 2010.

↶ My United States Geological Survey map of the Bristol Quadrangle is heavily seamed from so often being folded into backpacks or jacket pockets; its formerly white margin is soiled and splotched, its corners dog-eared. The street-grid of Bristol is shown in the southeastern corner of the map. But its central feature is the dramatic and heavily forested upland of the Hogback Ridge, running north-south and rising over a thousand feet above our village. Hogback is a finger of quartzite about ten miles long and between two and three miles across. Glaciation and erosion have stripped away the softer dolostones that once enclosed it within a higher plateau, sloughing them down to enrich the heavy clays to our west in the Champlain Valley. Hogback thus constitutes a resistant limb of bedrock and, although logged off several times over the past two centuries, has never been cultivated or settled. Our old house on North Street stands less than a quarter-mile from this roadless area enlivening the village with its wildness.

In walking out our backdoor to an outlook called the Ledges, from which I can look straight down at our house as well as clear across Addison County to Lake Champlain, I pass under a band of broad-branched, open-grown trees where wild turkeys often roost. They venture out to glean in nearby cornfields between harvest and the coming of the snow. In continuing my uphill hike, I enter thickening woods where evergreens are more prevalent. Deer trace their daily circuits here, bedding down under the hemlocks at night, while moose pass through on their way from the heights to the wetlands at the western edge of town. Farther up the slope comes a broken, rocky scramble of land where bobcats and black bears den.

Along with the various discolorations on its margin from tea and peanut- butter sandwiches held by fingers numb from the cold, there are two lines and an arrow which David drew onto my map in pencil. One of these traces the ridge of Hogback from the north to its southern terminus at a rugged cliff called Deer Leap, then angles west through the village. All of the land east and south of this line drains into the New Haven River as it runs through Bristol toward its meeting with Otter Creek and its ultimate destination in Lake Champlain. Much of the water washing down to the north and west of the ridge, however, will end up in Lewis Creek, which travels north into Hinesburg after its detour through Bristol Pond. On a cold afternoon in the February following my retirement from Middlebury College, David and I hiked up onto Hogback to figure out where the *rest* of the precipitation on the ridge ended up. We hoped to confirm his theory that there was a fan-shaped wedge of land on Hogback's western slope that intervened between the New

Haven and Lewis Creek drainages, ultimately conveying water due west along Plank Road into a tributary of the Little Otter Creek.

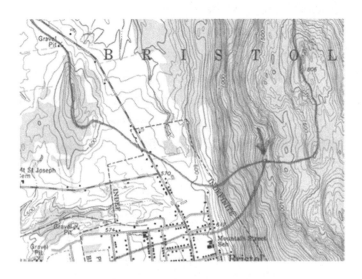

We climbed up from Mountain Street, passing through a tattery piece of wooded ground to the south of our destination. Map in hand, we wanted to locate a particular little knoll we believed might be just above us to the east. While far short of the height of country, it seemed from the map to be a possible location for the headwater of the Little Otter. We had little success at first, since most of the surface water was frozen into taut skins of ice the size of drumheads, silent and motionless until we crunched through them in our boots. At one point, though, as we stopped to listen to the world beyond our own motion, we heard bubbling. It came from a patch of cobbles lying with the looseness of talus and situated almost exactly at the place marked by an arrow on our map. In this part of Vermont, the temperature of ground-water holds at around 46 degrees Fahrenheit, so that springs can be discovered running in all seasons. This one spilled into a narrow, descending seam of land, establishing a watercourse that did indeed run directly west.

Standing immediately above that point of origin and division was a rugged granite erratic carpeted with common polypody, a robust and abundant fern in the Green Mountains. Kernels of snow from a recent storm nestled among its shriveled but still green fronds. Just up-slope from this landmark crossed an icy, treacherous road left over from a recent A. Johnson Company logging operation that had also left a hedge of slash along its track. The boulder we were concentrating on was about ten feet high and had steep sides. But we managed to scramble atop it. We'd tossed up a few rocks before making our grand ascent so that we could erect a commemorative cairn on a bare, level area of that ferny roof. A stack of three large flat stones established a statuary base of narrowing circumference, on which I set a rounder and more massive rock. Then we saw that a long tooth of ledge was already waiting for us on the erratic. One side of this triangular piece was cut away in a curve that let it tuck up smoothly beside and over the top of that round stone. It held steady there, a slender tip flickering above the cairn like a gray candle-flame.

After we had marveled at this providential balancing act, David got out a jar of maple syrup he'd brought along in a pocket of his timber cruiser's vest and dripped some of its dark, viscous contents down the sides of that crowning flame. It collected onto the stones below but also clung to and ambered the grainy surfaces of the vertical piece. We hoped that some rodent might happen upon this trove of calories and gain a chance to survive another Vermont winter.

↶ My Folding Landscapes map of Connemara, too, is far from pristine. Flecks of dried sphagnum moss tell the story of a subsequent foray into Roundstone Bog. I wanted to compare its catchments with those on the Hogback Ridge. These two largely roadless areas are similar in size as well as each being immediately adjacent to the center of a village. One heavily forested, the other nearly treeless, they are also alike in being easily explorable by classes from the local schools, by tourists who decide to set out for an afternoon hike after a slice of pizza at Cubber's in Bristol or a sandwich at Roundstone House, or by writers coming back day after day in search of the big picture. One place has been preserved from development through its steepness and rockiness, the other through its standing water and muck, but both offer portals into processes of self-renewal through which the meaning and potential of these rural communities too have evolved.

I intended to identify the catchments circulating through Roundstone Bog, just as David and I had done when climbing up the eastern side of Hogback. What I found, however, was that so much open water, surrounded by immense stretches of saturated sphagnum, kept me from discerning any clear sequence of watersheds comparable to that three-part division in Vermont. At one point I attempted to find my bearings by reconnoitering away from the sheep-trail I was following.

Plunging up to my waist in the mire, I feared I'd meet the Tollund Man's Irish cousin face-to-face before finally managing to wallow back to firm ground. Though I reached no clarity about catchments that day, it was still a lovely outing, with harriers gliding overhead, the northern horizon crenellated by the Twelve Pins, and graduated terraces cut into the trailside peat where turfs had been dug out in a way reminiscent of the staircase walls of Vermont's marble and granite quarries.

After many hours of poring over his map upon returning to Vermont, I finally resorted to emailing Tim Robinson to ask what *his* analysis of the Roundstone catchments was. He responded:

> Most of the area you mention drains through the Ballinaboy river to the NW, another good proportion of it through the Doohulla river to the SW, a marginal basin to the E is drained by a stream called Kelly's River (not named on the map). Since the relief is so subdued over most of this area the margins of the catchments must be very vague; there are indeed substantial surface streams linking long series of lakes, but there are level boggy patches in which the direction of flow could be determined by tiny accidents and interventions, mere oozings, droolings and snivelings marshaled one way or the other by a cow's hoofmark or a snipe's egg.

This message was a useful reminder not to give way to droolings and snivelings myself the next time I ventured, map in hand, into bogland.

↬ In a session Irish musicians often play two or three tunes together as a set. Someone starts up the first tune and, after companions familiar with it have played it through several times, nods to start the next piece. Typically, a given set's tunes are of the same type—reels, jigs, hornpipes, or marches. (Slow airs tend to be played by just one person, and not connected with another air.) Benedict Koehler and Hilari Farrington, in helping our workshop group become attuned to session-etiquette, as well as to the social pitfalls of an expanding and diversifying repertoire in our part of Vermont, suggest that if we're starting with a tune that might not be familiar to as many others in the circle it's often polite in moving on to make sure that the subsequent piece in the set is one that most people can easily join. A number of particular combinations can also become quite common in a given session or region, so that people naturally think of them together, almost as a single tune. Otherwise, as far as this neophyte can tell, there are no very strict rules about how sets are put together. Sometimes, but not always, they're in the same modal signature and may be quite similar in other ways as well. But it's entirely acceptable to go for a dramatic contrast between aspects of tunes as long as the second one holds to about the same pace as the first.

For me, Connemara and our part of Vermont form a *topographical* set. Not only are they two remarkably green realms of a certain size but they also lend themselves to walking at a similar pace, so that the rhythm of boots on one muddy trail can swing right into the next. When bushwhacking in Vermont one continually stumbles over root-mounds from the 1938 hurricane, while even on the Long Trail the going is syncopated by boulders, logs, and roots interrupting the path. On the occasions when flooding and muck drove me off the narrow way in Ireland I was likely to find myself hopping from hummock to hummock in a boggy expanse, and often enough pausing to pull out a foot that had sunk in over its boot-top. The herky-jerky nature of such outings put me in mind of the indomitable hornpipe "Pleasures of Hope" as I reconnoitered, skipped, and twisted my way across Roundstone's soggy reserve. And now, when playing this piece back home in Vermont, I'm still transported to that magnificent bog—in a spot of tune.

LINK:
The Pleaures
of Hope

I love the prevalence of triplets in hornpipes like "The Pleasures of Hope." They bring a rasty gusto to the tune, like an unembarrassed ham actor's operatic rolling of his r's. The ascending triplet with which this tune begins immediately descends again through arpeggios to a roll on F#. The effect for me, as it was with all those rolls on G and A that I came to love in "The Trip to Birmingham," is of *music* that bubbles. The ebullience bursting through this simple melody is like laughter that both disrupts and fulfills a conversation between old friends. Such a tune can also become the occasion for hilarious inventiveness, both in ornamentation and in a constant game of rephrasing from one time through to the next. Sometimes the close resemblance between tunes in a set allows such variations to unspool like endless variations on a theme.

I can also think of lots of other hornpipes beginning with

the same triplet leaping up to D that then go off in quite different directions. One of these that Rita and I like to play in a set with "The Pleasures of Hope" is "The Fairy Queen," which ends up having a much more whimsical feeling. The way in which they start in identical fashions then veer apart, just as a player might be getting secure with their resemblance, gives these two hornpipes an *uncanny* similarity, like Connemara and Vermont—kindred landscapes yet with such important differences. In their fractured parallels they make me think of Benedict Koehler's advice that in memorization people always need to keep an eye out for an approaching "fork in the road." As Frost has written, a certain bewilderment, sometimes bordering on paralysis, can result from encountering so many turnings and departures: "Two paths diverged in a yellow wood, /And knowing I could not travel both/And be one traveler, long I stood . . ." The only way across a threshold of this sort may be to step forward impulsively. If a new ornament, phrasing, or set turns out to work well, we may return to it. One way or another, as in Rita's and my impulse to take up Irish music in the first place, the significance of our choices may become clear only in retrospect.

The strong similarities among many Irish melodies both create a powerful sense of tradition and make even more dramatic the real differences between both tunes and performers. When two tunes start exactly alike, as "The Pleasures of Hope" and "The Fairy Queen" do, you will have one in your ears while playing the other. Part of the fun of a session can come from such unplanned experiences of shared associations and collaborative memory, as similar motifs and flavors carry one tune into another as slickly as a rising triplet. I'm reminded in this connection of the profound simplicity of Japan's haiku tradition. Though these brief poems avoid complexity or elaboration on their surfaces, they gain depth through their strong associations with other haiku. Just as the opening of "The Pleasures of Hope" recurs in other hornpipes, *furuike ya* ("old pond"), the opening syllables of Bash's most famous haiku, have been carried over into the opening lines of numerous other haiku as well. Variations on a theme naturally assume prominence in traditions that on some level celebrate rural simplicity.

⤳ In comparison with a USGS topo map, Robinson's cartography has a strikingly open quality. There's no color scheme of white for low ground, green for mountainous terrain, and blue for water. Rather than using dark brown contour lines, like the ones that swirl and gather when elevations quickly rise in maps of the Green Mountains, Robinson simply indicates contours with fine broken lines. His intention, as opposed to overlaying schematic information onto the landscape, is to scour off the blurry surface of the Connemara palimpsest. He wants to rake away the topographic gravel deposited over the past century and a half so that the springs may run clear again and the holy wells may be revealed. One of the ways he manages this, having started out with the official Ordnance Survey maps, is to dispense with as many of the superimposed English place names as possible—substituting the Irish names that he has painstakingly recovered through a combination of bibliographic research and conversations with elderly, Irish-speaking neighbours. Names and stories, not simply rainfall, bring exactness to the map of Connemara's catchments.

A reader who unfolds a copy of Robinson's map while standing atop Errisbeg, the 917-foot-high promontory rising at the southeastern edge of Roundstone Bog, will note that this map's primary identification for that peak is the older name *Iorras Beag*, meaning "small peninsula" in Irish. Such a return to the earlier name both establishes its historical primacy and suggests a characteristic and indigenous way of responding to the land. Mountains are not separate from and exalted over low places. Rather, they are simply the most visible manifestations of a larger area from which they derive a meaning and identity much more significant than the mere fact of elevation. Both the mountain and its southern skirts have been named, it seems, for the Goirtín Peninsula, which lies due south of Iorras Beag and southeast along the coast from Roundstone Bay.

In the *Gazetteer* Tim Robinson published to accompany his map, he elaborates on the peninsula's name, "*Goirtín*/small plot. A fine tombolo or neck of foraminiferous sand links this islet to the mainland; the deposits of seashells and the darker levels of soil visible in the faces of the eroded dunes here and on the tombolo represent ancient (perhaps Neolithic) settlement levels." For both the native Connemaran and the visitor just being introduced to Ireland and its ancient place names, the deeply historical character of this etymology has a strong appeal. As the dunes of imperial history erode, they also disclose. A midden of language is exposed beneath the sandy years, allowing a hiker who carries this map to imagine centuries of forerunners in the misty, windswept vastness of the bog, including some who made it their home long before all recorded histories of this turbulent place.

The Ordnance Maps with which Tim Robinson began were highly accurate with respect to the scalloped indentation of coastlines as well as to the location of towns and mountains. As Brian Friel's play *Translations* conveys, however, the creation of these maps in the early part of the nineteenth-century saw the introduction of many misleading place names. Surveying parties were sent out under the leadership of officers in the Royal Engineers to take stock of the Empire's Hibernian real estate. But many of the names they came up with were either inept attempts to translate the Irish names' meanings or transliterations of their sound by cartographers who knew no Gaelic. The overall effect was one of effacement, since the long-established Irish names had often carried with them mythical, historical, and familial narratives that spun and wove a living web of stories in the land.

In *Listening to the Wind*, Robinson never loses sight of the damage caused when such deep cultural continuity with the land is lost. As he says at one point, "Irish placenames dry out when anglicized, like twigs snapped off from a tree." A place may become more vulnerable to exploitation when bereft of a deeply rooted name that pointed to its natural characteristics and recalled its history. Ecological and social withering can follow from linguistic desiccation. Robinson's insistence on indigenous place names, in his writing and on his maps alike, has sent me back to the topo map for the Bristol Quadrangle with new eyes. There are in fact almost no place names of any kind on the map of Hogback and its catchments. English names from the nearby towns of Bristol, Starksboro, Hinesburg, and Monkton nibble around its edges, while the New Haven River is prominently labeled as it wraps around Deer Leap. But with the other exceptions of the Ledges and the tributaries flowing down into the Champlain Valley, the many plateaus, cliffs, boulder fields, and vernal pools that are landmarks for hikers within Hogback's dramatically contorted terrain go nameless on the map.

Residents in this part of Vermont who are of European descent are impoverished by a general oblivion to the names and stories woven into the land over many centuries by the Western Abenaki—just as the original people's descendants here are also disenfranchised by their neighbors' ignorance. In contrast to other parts of North America where Indian place names are commonly used and large local tribes persist, many Abenaki withdrew into Québec because of the frequent armed conflicts in the region during the latter part of the eighteenth century. Those who did remain, after European settlers arrived in large numbers around the beginning of the nineteenth-century, encountered prejudice and hostility that often led them to disguise their identity.

I would not propose a complete parallel between the histories of indigenous naming in Vermont and Connemara. The Irish reasserted control over their land and language many years ago, while the Abenaki people's four bands in Vermont have only been officially recognized by the state within the last few years. Still, Tim Robinson's dedication to helping recover the earlier place names of Connemara convinces me that a fuller sense of affiliation with this northeastern corner of Addison County will require all citizens to learn more about the original Abenaki names for this landscape. A commitment to one's place on earth must be both a daily practice and a broadening of cultural awareness. Joseph Bruchac's collections of traditional Abenaki stories have proven essential to me in forging such a connection close to home, as has Kevin Dann's excellent local history *Lewis Creek Lost and Found*.

Another good starting point for such a pursuit might be with those catchments on the slope above Bristol. In the work of an ethnographer named Gordon Day, I find that Otter Creek was called *Pecunktuk*, or the Crooked River, in Abenaki. The Little Otter was known as *Wonakakituk*, or the River of Otters, while the Lewis Creek was *Sungahnetuk*, the Fishing Place—or perhaps the River of Fish Weirs, with reference to stones placed there in order to form enclosures where fish might be taken. Our Addison County friend and neighbor Pete Sutherland has composed numerous songs about this part of Vermont that incorporate Abenaki and Québécois place names. His repetition of *Wonakakituk* definitely brings a snappy pulse to the refrain of his song called "The Indian Road"! The name of Alaska's Mt. McKinley, the highest peak in North America, has already reverted to its Native name of Denali, thus scraping away the detritus of a third-rate president's surname and restoring the grandeur of its original Koyukon title, the High One. But Tim Robinson's example suggests the necessity for a sustained process of recovery extending even to more modest locales like Hogback—carried out with the same patience required for tracing the thousands of rivulets in a catchment.

Such an effort of attentiveness to the testimony of elderly residents in suppressed communities, while essential to both greater groundedness and greater fairness, can also sound an elegiac note. "In noting such almost obliterated communal memories," Robinson writes, "I sometimes feel like a priest bending his ear to the mouth of a dying man to capture the profound and determinative sense of his last breath." Reverence is at the heart of Robinson's view of history and the land. Not reverence for a transcendental truth, but rather a compassionate and deeply respectful concern for how people worked and carried on in the face of a challenging environment and under the heel of rapacious invaders. When elegy reaches deep enough to touch the bedrock of history, it arrives at a tragic perspective on survival in the land. Accordingly, as Robinson has written, it is "wrong to treat the Famine as just a period. It was in fact the keystone in a triumphal arch of suffering . . . There has never been a year in which it would have been appropriate to celebrate the end of the famine; instead, it has been forgotten while the ragged edges of its shadow still lie around our feet." History, in a wounded landscape, can feel like a haunting—the embedded presence of so much that might have seemed lost. Ireland's music too feels haunted, for me, in its shadowed but indomitable quality. On the sketchy paths of Errisbeg and Hogback, as well, I have walked into a shared rhythm of abandonment and persistence—one established not only by human history, but also long before that in an intriguing geological parallel between the two regions.

↪ The mapping of catchments and the tracking of tectonic plates as they drift across the mantle with their cargo of continents both require attention to the rocky surface of the earth. Despite their striking differences of spatial and temporal scale, these are both physical phenomena whose evidence and effects are apparent everywhere. Tim Robinson's knowledge of geology not only infuses his readings of the surface and history of our planet with drama but also provides a context for understanding broad shifts and continuities in the realms of ecology and culture. Here is how, in a late chapter of *Listening to the Wind* entitled "Walking the Skyline," he describes a band of rocks near the Twelve Pins:

> These rocks are of schist and marble; that is, they are of clayey and limey materials originally deposited in layers on an ocean floor and later metamorphosed and upended by geological forces. The Dalradian ocean in which they were born once stretched from what is now the Shetlands to the west of Ireland, and it lay within a vast supercontinent that comprised most of the Earth's present land masses, for this was long before the Atlantic came into existence. . . . Eventually the stretching and rifting of the continental plate culminated in the birth of the Iapetus Ocean, the predecessor of the Atlantic, which lasted for some 100 million years and began to close up again around 510 million years ago. The Dalradian sedimentary rocks were caught up in the reunion of the continents; they were crumpled and torn, pushed down into the hot depths of the Earth and thrust up into mountain chains of Himalayan proportions.

Just as every point on the surface of the earth is situated within a specific local catchment, so too all parts of the landscape are borne along on tectonic plates that collide from epoch to epoch, raising new mountain ranges from deposits on the continental shelves that are collected, compressed, and lifted up as the edge of one plate slides up over that of another. In this regard, I was fascinated to discover another concrete connection between Ireland and Vermont when I set aside my Bristol topo and the Folding Landscapes "Connemara" in order to lay two *bedrock* maps of the regions side by side. They had been made up for me by Ray Coish, who teaches Geology at Middlebury College. I took the rubber bands off the long, rolled-up maps and anchored them on my study floor with books at the corners so that I could stand above them and take a long view.

These maps revealed a remarkable correlation between the bedrocks of Connemara and the Green Mountains. The intricate mix of rocks in the Dalradian Schist Robinson describes is closely replicated in the composition of schists in the mountains of Vermont. Such a similarity is neither a simple coincidence nor a common sort of parallel. Instead, it reflects a shared geological origin. Just to the east of present-day Lake Champlain (which defines the western boundary of Vermont for about half of our state's 159-mile length) there once lay a continental shelf. When the Iapetus Ocean began to close, as Robinson relates, it folded together and compressed the sediments on that shelf, raising them into mountains that were the much higher ancestors of today's Green Mountains and the Appalachian chain to which they belong. They rose near the middle of a great supercontinent called Pangaea.

When Pangaea in its turn began to break up and the Atlantic Ocean to open, approximately 130 million years ago, a new line of separation lay to the *east* of the earlier shore. The Appalachians were pulled apart, with one remaining ridge running down from Newfoundland through New England and the Carolinas to Georgia. Other parts of the range migrated eastward with the European Plate. Millions of years of erosion, including major episodes of glaciation, have effaced much of the mountain chain in Europe, while also lowering it significantly in North America. But the remaining bedrock shows striking similarities between Connemara and the Green Mountains, both in overall composition and in the specific, intricate sequence of mineralogical bands that organizes the two landscapes.

Just before Pangaea began disassembling itself into separate continents and drifting apart, Newfoundland and Ireland were directly attached to one another. Their bedrock maps are thus absolutely identical. But the geological parallels between Vermont and Connemara also remain quite striking, except in one regard. On the geological map of Ireland, the schist in the center of Connemara is composed of east-west bands of the various Dalradian Appin and Argyll Groups, as well as of the Killary-Joyces Succession; these are represented on my map by a bracing shuffle of emerald, fuchsia, pink, brown, and violet. But the bands in Vermont, which exactly align with the orientation of the Green Mountains, appear as north-south on the map. When the Iapetus was closing to form the Appalachians, the coastline of the North American, or Laurentian, plate curved dramatically, which led to a similar change of orientation in the mountain chain formed along its shelf. Thus, today's Appalachian bedrock, after heading north and then northeast through New England and Newfoundland, turns almost due east through parts of Ireland, Wales, and England before resuming a northeastern course into Scotland and Norway. Portions of the original mountain system also ended up in the Netherlands, coastal France, and northwestern Spain.

Such a family resemblance, geologically speaking, reinforces my growing interest in Irish music. It also accords with the progression of my own life, from birth in Kentucky to adulthood in Vermont, up the Appalachian spine towards Newfoundland. The fretless banjo, my first "folk" instrument, has like my classical instrument the French horn, given way for me to playing Irish flute. Even before observing those colorful Appalachian bedrocks splashed into the maps of Ireland and Vermont, I was struck (as many others have also been) by the strong continuities between Celtic musical traditions and those of the southern Appalachians and New England. Many of the same tunes have been played on both sides of the Atlantic since the middle of the eighteenth century. In another intriguing connection to their identical bedrock, Newfoundland is often described as the most Irish place outside of Ireland, as well as being the only one with its own name in Irish—*Talamh an Eisc*, or "the fishing ground." When I asked Ray Coish, a native Newfie, if there was much Irish music played where his family came from he said in his understated way, "Well, we call it Newfoundland music."

It's intriguing to contemplate such musical continuity within a tradition that, while not confined to any one country, is strongly associated with certain rocky landscapes that resist easy cultivation. A haunting heritage is transmitted through modal structures that can madden amiable guitar players who try to join in with their standard chord progressions. Right up through such Celtic offspring as bluegrass, there's a *keening* quality in the music, as melodies break across ancient droning shores.

For the growing number of Celtic music's devotees who live far from the Appalachian arch, including many in Western and Eastern Europe, Russia, Japan, Australia, and New Zealand, the music also seems to express a longing for values too often neglected in the modern conversation of nations. Though few people are likely to have settled in the rocky, depopulated reaches of Connemara or the Green Mountains primarily because of a desire to get rich, many who have been "in populous city pent" long for the strategic retreat to rootedness and away from consumerism that such places seem to represent. For them, ancient tunes like "Langstrom's Pony" that don't fit meekly into a standard key, convey this liberating contrast. The bedrocks of the Champlain Valley Belt, Green Mountain Belt, and Rowe-Hawley Belt that flow from the chambered heart of Connemara down the length of Vermont have no causal relation to the fiddle, flute, banjo, concertina, and pipe music now connecting our two regions. But the similar tunes played in both are nonetheless tokens of something more essential to our sense of place than the products lining the shelves of big-box stores or the sizzling urgency of news flashes on the television or the computer.

In chasing this musical rabbit, I've veered off the page of Tim Robinson's majestic and highly localized precision. Despite the melodic cadences and fricative rhythms that bring such music to his prose, there's no getting around this warning lodged near the beginning of the Preface: "History has rhythms, tunes and even harmonies; but the sound of the past is an agonistic multiplicity. Sometimes, rarely, a scrap of a voice can be caught from the universal damage, but it may only be an artefact of the imagination, a confection of rumours." How easily can a reflection puff up into a confection. Indeed, my earlier remark that Robinson's writing invites inhabitants of other hinterlands to lay their maps edge to edge with his was not quite right either. The vitality of his book is like that of a catchment. It is a system to be observed, walked around, and returned to: neither a doorway nor a staircase that might lead away from Connemara. Yet for all that, his fierce attention to overlooked places that have temporarily lost their names remains "profoundly suggestive of a way of looking at the world and caring for it." Time to brush last spring's sphagnum off the map and climb back up Errisbeg.

Ecotones

LANGSTROM PONY

Over a dozen years ago Rita and I met with a local financial advisor named Christine Moriarty. (Since this was before the beginning of my interest in all things Irish, my immediate association with her name was with that of Sherlock Holmes's nemesis.) Christine's special focus was working with women at moments of transition in their lives when some careful planning about money was required. But she was perfectly happy to talk with us as a couple about when retirement might be in the cards, economically speaking. After she had looked over all our pertinent information about income, savings, and indebtedness, we set up a conference at our home. Her simple message was, "Sure. Retirement in your sixties should definitely be possible as long as you plan on staying pretty frugal."

She also recommended, however, that we think of retirement as three chapters of our life, not one. In her observation, the first episode for many people, right after leaving full-time employment, was an opportunity to pursue a number of longed-for projects they just hadn't found time for in the past. Travel, learning a new language, participation in service projects, and carrying out ambitious reading programs were typical activities for such new retirees. After a few years, however, when they'd already accomplished a lot of those deferred goals, they generally found themselves entering a second phase. They now preferred to settle down into more sedate enjoyment of their own homes: tending their gardens, playing with their grandchildren, and relishing the opportunity for regular naps and leisurely meals. "Then comes the third and final stage," she said, like Jaques wrapping up his Seven Ages of Man speech in *As You Like It*, "when you're feeling old and sick and nothing's much fun anymore."

The bleakness of Christine's third chapter gave credibility to the earlier, sunnier elements of her overview. From visiting my grandmother and my father in the nursing home that was their final berth, I already recognized that the end of a long life can be difficult and distressing. Though a passage that can certainly be navigated with grace, it's still not generally a situation to be longed for. One conclusion Rita and I both drew from this play in three acts was that we'd like to expand the *first* of retirement's phases! As it happens, our shared musical pursuits, related travels to Ireland, visits to her relatives outside of Rome, and road trips catching up with friends we hadn't enjoyed enough time with in recent years have all ratified Christine's hopeful sense of retirement's beginnings.

Despite such pleasures, though, this first phase of retirement still feels primarily like a transitional interval for me, in which I have one foot in my vocational landscape of reading, teaching, and writing, the other in the less sponsored terrain of home, Hogback, and Irish music. I do not expect to make my way through this zone with the confidence I attained as a teacher at Middlebury, or to play the flute as well as I once played the horn. Similarly, though I frequently still lace up my hiking boots to explore the nearby woods, I move more slowly now and carry trekking poles. But the chance to look both backward and forward from this successional vantage point makes it feel like not only a new adventure but also a rich and surprising harvest. Everything that was, still is—yet refreshed and interestingly strange through being so closely interwoven with other, altered circumstances.

One analogy for this transition from my career at the college is a gradually shifting orientation to home I have often observed in Middlebury sophomores. In holidays during their freshman year and in the summer vacation following it, students are typically avid to return to their hometowns and hang out with their high school friends. During the second year, however, the new friends they've made, and the studies and extracurricular activities that have come to occupy them at college, make going home on breaks, while perhaps still pleasant, an interruption of their primary and preferred reality. I'm like those sophomores now, at the point just before their decisive shift of orientation. With the passage of a bit more time, I imagine, the intensity of Middlebury, the books I taught there, and the students I worked with so closely will begin to fade. But for now, as I hike up among the glacial erratics of Hogback on a mild day that makes it feel safe to carry my flute case in the backpack along with my lunch, the writers I've loved continue to accompany me step by step.

↜ Ecologists speak of "edge-effect" as prevailing along the boundaries between two ecosystems. Such transitional habitats, known as ecotones or ecoclines, are often remarkably rich environments. They can contain highly diverse collections of species, with some creatures and plants originating in each of the adjacent ecosystems and others unique to the edge itself. Their biotic mass also tends to be much greater than that of the surrounding habitats. This concept of ecotones, which long influenced my approach to interdisciplinary teaching, now helps me recognize the potential in retirement as well. At the threshold between full-time teaching and our new dedication to Irish music, Rita and I have encountered just such a proliferation of experiences and discoveries.

I've started thinking of this chapter of our life as an ecotone because of its marked quality of *betweenness*. Retirement situates Rita and me more decisively in Bristol, on its narrow alluvial plateau between the broad fields of the Champlain Valley and the rocky buttresses of Mount Abraham. Even as I have gained more time for playing Irish tunes and walking in the hills, authors like Wordsworth and Woolf, Frost and Silko have continued speaking in my mind every day. Their words are entangled with all those tunes. My trajectory into this ecotone has been uphill and to the east, and as I forge farther in I experience another aspect of edge-effect. Namely, that there are always edges within edges, with a given ecotone being more of a striated band than a simple line. In areas near one side or the other the collection of species may closely resemble those in the adjacent ecosystem, while closer to its middle inhabitants unique to the ecotone may become prevalent. As Frost's idea of mountain intervals similarly implies, one's life moves both into and *through* such a rich but narrow zone. Energy is generated from such a passage which then, as with Robinson's catchments, flows outward into some larger system of confluence.

At the center of my own mountain interval, and of my experience of picking up the flute, has been our old clapboard house on Bristol's North Street. This is where we raised Rachel, Matthew, and Caleb, and where we continued to manage the stairs to the second floor now that we were the only ones sleeping there. Retirement changed our relationship with this two-century-old structure, though. Before, it was the snug harbor to which members of the family returned from our various schools every evening. In my own case most days were spent on the manicured campus of Middlebury College, with its stately granite and marble buildings. Middlebury, the Shiretown for Addison County, is set amid the rolling fields of one of New England's most prosperous agricultural regions. It's the hub of commerce and the location of the local courthouse and hospital as well as being the home of Vermont's oldest and wealthiest college.

At this point, however, the scrappy mountain town of Bristol, where farms have always been less important to the local economy than forestry, is where I find myself. One point of reference for me now is the perpetually peeling house and the large yard where no grounds crew sweeps in to collect fallen branches and rake gravel kicked up by the snowplows back into the street come spring. Another is the Hogback Ridge, whose exposed ledges, half an hour above our side porch, offer a view of our whole village. Around this vantage point spreads a third-growth forest of maple, beech, and white pine, while above it rises a bouldery slope where bear tracks are imprinted in the exposed and muddy ground of spring.

This shaggy world is the topography of my retirement. It is not affiliated with any large, prosperous institution, as I no longer am myself. Its economy (like mine now) is also considerably less robust than the college's. From time to time there are open storefronts on Bristol's Main Street, like the missing teeth of certain neighbors who could have profited from more time with a dentist. (Our one dentist in Bristol pulled up roots to resettle in Middlebury quite a few years back, though in just the past year a couple of new practices have finally been implanted here.) I was now spending many mornings in the upstairs study that was once Matthew's bedroom, typing away with a quilt over my legs. Not much heat from our woodstove in the living room ever wound its way up the stairs and through the two intervening rooms to the recliner where I sat. My shoulders and knees still ache occasionally from the polymyalgia that hit me right after retirement. Because I have now largely recovered from it, there is yet another reason to identify with the wounded and recovering slope just to our east. Off the payroll and up the hill to Bristol I've come, to remap the landscape of my life and play the flute.

 ↬ Edges within edges. Within Ireland's traditional repertoire itself one experiences the juxtaposition of traditional country dances with the forms and melodies of music's Baroque Era. Between those two habitats proliferated the artful and innovative, but also informal and sociable, ecotone of Irish traditional music. Turlough O'Carolan, the blind harper and creator of such beloved tunes as "Shebeg Shemore" and "Planxty Fanny Power," is an intriguing edge figure from this era. He was both a Baroque composer in his own right and a musician firmly planted in the Irish idiom. Our musical companion and friend John Murray, who immigrated to Vermont from Ireland, generally refuses to play O'Carolan tunes. To him they feel too self-conscious and premeditated for one thing. Besides, he objects to the fact that O'Carolan often supported himself by playing and composing for the landowners of the Protestant Ascendancy, who had supplanted much of the native Irish aristocracy. We sometimes tease John that he's being pretty hard on a blind old harper who was just trying to make a living in a tough neighborhood! Even as a lover of O'Carolan, though, I appreciate John's passionate and historically grounded response to the music. Tension and conflict often do mark an edge.

Danger, too. Ecologically and otherwise, edges are always moving. The first important teacher about ecology to a worldwide audience was Rachel Carson, whose primary reference as a scientist and writer was often to the edge of the sea. Carson (our daughter Rachel's namesake) was especially fascinated by the tide pools of her beloved Maine coast. These dynamic ecotones support both marine and terrestrial organisms as well as being crucial resources for birds. Twice a day they are exposed to the air, before becoming deeply submerged again. In order to benefit from such extraordinarily nutritious zones, creatures venturing in from time to time must be opportunistic and alert, while those living most of their lives in such ecotones must be tough enough to withstand the pounding of surf against rock.

Irish history, too, has been a stony shoreline beset by rough surf. Even before the Elizabethan suppression, with the centuries of poverty and violence that followed it, Irish Sagas have described wave after wave of invasions. Marie Heaney sums up these deep mythical and historical accounts as "Nine Waves." Certain former victors, now overthrown, still harbor sullenly and dangerously just below the surface of the Irish land. Such a story of nonstop contention and insecurity accords with the surfy rhythms and blustery tones pulsing through the traditional music. Classical music as we know it today prizes consistent, glowing tones in the instruments of the orchestra. But this preference has primarily been a development of the past two centuries. Take my old instrument the French horn. Right through the Classical and Romantic Eras, orchestras called for the hand horn or Waldhorn. Using the lip plus adjustments by the right hand, which was held in the horn's bell, skilled musicians could attain a pretty good chromatic scale.

To go from key to key horn players simply inserted crooks that lengthened or shortened the total column of air. Knowing which notes in a particular key would require almost complete hand-stopping, composers could incorporate that buzzy timbre into their overall conception of the sound. Brahms, who was a master of writing for the horn, lived when valves began to be introduced. At first they were employed simply to avoid all those crooks, but pretty soon people also began using them to avoid the different timbres of the hand horn; they wanted every tone to be ring clear. Brahms preferred the previous range of sound and resisted this change, specifying that only valveless horns should be used for his own compositions. But he couldn't stem the tide turning toward a conception of bright beauty for all the instruments of the orchestra.

The flute is in fact another dramatic example of this change. Theobald Boehm revolutionized the flute in the first half of the nineteenth-century by manufacturing silver instruments that were more durable and less variable in the weather, by adding a raised portion around the embouchure hole to promote greater consistency in the wind stream, by switching from a conical bore to a cylindrical one, and by designing a system of interlocking keys controlling the pads over all of the holes for individual notes. Even though Boehm flutes are beautiful for both looking at and listening to, here too something was lost through such modernization. Wooden flutes sound, well, woodier—producing a distinctive, warm tone. They can sound shoreline rough, too. A player's fingers rest on six open holes—quite large ones that allow for bending a note by sliding rather than simply lifting a fingertip. The lack of a raised area around the embouchure hole also allows for a dramatic variety of tones to be produced. When I first began to play the flute, Brad Hurley told me to envision splitting my stream of air at the farther edge of the hole. He also recommended *pushing* the sound a bit so that low notes were always quivering right at the edge of jumping up an octave. Such a vibrant tone quality allows the D, which is an Irish flute's lowest note, to "bark" in ways that energize a tune and lend a striking effect when (as is often the case) that also turns out to be a piece's final note.

⌐ Venturing into an ecotone is a gamble for any pioneer from one of the adjacent worlds. Though lured in by the promise of bounty, a creature tiptoeing in may end up being lunch for a hungry fellow-immigrant arriving from the opposite direction. An extra burst of speed, or special alertness to strange shadows gliding over the grass, may turn out to be necessary in such an unfamiliar environment. As a former French horn player picking up the flute I soon realized that I too would now need a higher level of alertness. In particular, I would need to become much more attentive to the underlying harmonies of Irish music.

My technical focus with the horn had been on making beautiful legato transitions from one note to the next, and on constantly tuning such intervals through adjustments with my lip and with my right hand in the bell. But I never received much training in music theory. French horn players, like tenors, tend to be scarce on the ground and we sometimes push our luck. A hornist's duty was to sit as decorously as possible in the back row of the orchestra, to transpose fairly reliably from the various keys in which orchestral parts for horn are still often printed, to strive for a floating, lyrical tone in all our exposed passages, and to steer away from "clams," or horribly cracked notes in the upper register. If we could accomplish all those things (or even just two or three of them) no one would push us too hard for either a knowledge of musical theory or altogether excellent behavior as we collaborated in counting our many measures of rests.

By contrast, Rita, as a pianist, was thoroughly schooled in scales, keys, and chordal progressions, and has always been a wonderful in-house resource on all matters harmonic. It reflects badly on me to admit this, but only after we were married and playing chamber music together did I learn all the names of keys determined by the sharps or flats on the staff. None of either: key of C. Just a B-flat: key of F. An F-sharp and a C-sharp: key of D. I was absurdly pleased to master these minor technical matters most self-respecting musicians would have learned in elementary school. I hung in there, too, when she schooled me on the difference between major keys (with a full tone differential between adjacent notes of an octave, except for the half-tones between the third and fourth notes and the seventh and eighth) and minor keys (where the half-steps shifted to between the second and third and the sixth and seventh notes). There. Now I could go back to my high-school psychology of passing notes in the back row as we horn players awaited our next glorious entrance.

When becoming serious about Irish music, however, I suddenly needed to grasp the relationships between *modes* in addition to those between various standard major and minor keys. Furthermore, my brain was much older now than when I was first tutored by my lovely young chamber-music coach. It required concentration in order to understand, for instance, that a key-signature showing sharps in F# and C# did _not_ necessarily indicate the key of D. Everything depended on how the melody was draped across a given octave and where the half-note intervals appeared. My initial struggles with this shifting musical reality reminded me of the passage in Annie Dillard's essay "Total Eclipse" when she describes her grasp of astronomy as being "so frail that, given a flashlight, a grapefruit, two oranges, and fifteen years, we still could not figure out which way to set the clocks for Daylight Saving Time."

Rita invited me to sit to her left on the bench of the Steinway piano she'd inherited from her grandfather Cesare Cianfoni, a musician who immigrated from Italy and made his living, first in Pennsylvania and then in California, as a composer, conductor, and vocal coach. She placed my right hand with the thumb on middle C, and had me play all the white keys in that octave. This initial mode, called the Ionian, was also in fact C-major. Early in our marriage, she had given piano lessons in our house on North Street, and I delighted now in being the overgrown pupil whose hand she moved up and down the keys. Next she positioned it so that the thumb was on the D and had me do the same thing, still sticking only to the white keys. In continuing to ascend the keyboard I was sounding out the Dorian, Phrygian, Lydian, Mixolydian, Aeolian (equivalent to what are commonly known as minor keys), and Locrian modes, respectively. With each new starting note, the two half-note intervals shifted to different locations within a given mode.

In his _Essential Guide to Irish Flute and Tin Whistle_ Gray Larsen points out, however, that almost all Irish music is confined to the Ionian, Dorian, and Mixolydian modes. That came as a relief to me. He also emphasizes the importance of keeping track of a given mode's "tonal center," since focusing on "each note's intervallic relationship to it will greatly enhance your ability to learn, internalize, and remember tunes." Accordingly, he advocates thinking of a "mode signature," like A-Mixolydian, when that mode continually returns to A, in order to keep from assuming that with a key signature of F# and C# this would be a tune in D major. I realize in writing about all this, however, that I need to ask Rita to talk it through with me again. Be that as it may, here's what the Ionian, Dorian, and Mixolyidian modes sound like on the flute

LINK: *Common Irish Modes*

Modal music often sounds *ancient*. The tune that for me sums up this dark and emotional element within the Irish tradition is "Langstrom Pony." This is a jig I learned from Chris Norman at the Potomac Valley Piper's Gathering. Sessions were offered on the Great Highland bagpipes, the more parlor-friendly Scottish smallpipes, the Northumbrian pipes, and Ireland's Uilleann pipes. Participants purchased long-sleeve T-shirts featuring the portrait of a soulful hound-dog wrapped around a set of Uillean pipes under the Gathering's official motto: "Squeeze the Bag." Pipers often play the flute or whistle, which means that there are also typically workshops and lessons for those instruments. I traveled down to this Gathering in Shepardstown, West Virginia in order to take a couple of private flute lessons with Chris Norman as well as attend his workshops on Irish, Scottish, and Cape Breton repertoire.

Classically trained at the Indiana University School of Music and having played in Baltimore's early music consort for a number of years, Chris Norman subsequently shifted his musical base of operations back to his native Nova Scotia and founded the Boxwood Festival there. He cultivates an interest in Irish, Scottish, Cape Breton, and Québécois music alike. Irish music remains at the core of this tradition for Rita and me, but the fact that my own heritage is largely Highland Scots on my father's side and entirely Scotch-Irish on my mother's made me eager to learn about this wider musical heritage. In addition, Québec is of course a strong cultural influence here in northern Vermont, with Montréal by far our closest major city. This reality, in addition to the fact that my paternal grandmother Thérèse Richard was a Cajun with roots in New Brunswick when it was still part of l'Acadie, has also fed a growing interest in the essentially Celtic music of francophone Canada.

Chris Norman's broad musical background seems to dispose him to flexibility and variety in interpreting Celtic music. Such an orientation also expresses his sense of its evolutionary expansion from certain common roots, including the pervasive influence of baroque music in the seventeenth and eighteenth centuries. Within such a conceptual framework, he introduced our group to "Langstrom Pony," a tune that remains a landmark for me. Because it's a jig in A-Mixolydian it alternates between triads in A and in G alternatively. Chris called such a tone "drone-based," because it rocks back and forth as opposed to circling through a progression of chords. He also remarked that such a quality of primal simplicity was typical of many especially old tunes. In fact, he said "Langstrom Pony" was one of a small number of "super tunes," that serve as "transit points" where "data collects" from various musical traditions.

There are versions of the song in Ireland (the one he taught us) as well as in Scotland, in English country-dance music, and in Brittany. The strange title may be one token of the tune's remote and mysterious origins, and at the bottom of one photocopied version he passed out after we'd learned the tune by ear a number of competing names were listed: "Langstrom Pony, The Langstern Pony, Langstram Pony, Lostrum Ponia, Lanstrum Poney, Lanxtrum Pony, Lastrum Pony, Lastrum Pone, Saddle the Pony . . ."

Since first learning tunes by ear in Catherine McEvoy's workshop, I've come to love the process because of the way its necessary slowness and repetition emphasize simple patterns that ascend and descend through the range of an instrument, inverting, contrasting, and otherwise answering each other in ways that seem like the chromosomal spiraling of genes. When I was in college I started piano one semester, then had to give it up for lack of time. I've always remembered with fondness, though, my teacher's assigning me weekly exercises from Béla

Bartok's *Mikrokosmos*. These extremely simple études traced the permutations and combinations within a small cluster of notes in a way I found entrancing. I have a similar feeling of being

LINK: *Langstrom Pony*

transported when I play "Langstrom Pony," causing me both to return to it often and to play it over and over once I have gotten started.

↪ In our workshops Chris Norman emphasized the value of playing tunes slowly even after one has memorized them, in order both to explore how they might unfold interpretively and to play around with ornamentation while never losing the solid rhythm. "Langstrom Pony," as a jig, should generally move along in a bouncy fashion. But playing it more slowly, as I still often like to do, makes the recurrent shifting down from A to G, as well as the substitution of a C-natural for the previous C-sharps, feel even more deliciously, weird. It sounds like Dali's melting pocket-watch looks, offering moments of vertigo such as when, with my mind elsewhere, I find one more (or one less) step than I was expecting when descending the stairs. One version of the tune Chris shared with us at the class's conclusion is called "Lastrumpony" and consists of ten repeated sections. Since most tunes just have an A and a B part, this proliferation of sections is a further strangeness—a set of variations that feels like a meandering excursion through the watershed of one super-tune.

Playing more slowly can also help focus a player's attention on breathing in the right places. In classical music the general practice is to breathe at the end of a phrase. But in class Chris Norman teased me about my horn player's tendency to rush a quick breath after one of a jig's quick triplets. For a listener whose ear is attuned to the Celtic tradition, such a practice undermines what should the *strong* note at the beginning of the next three eighth notes. Rather than sneaking in a breath, it's thus much preferable to find notes to leave out, and that have the effect of reinforcing a piece's fundamental rhythm and shape. In Catherine McEvoy's recordings it's fun listening to the segments of tunes when she turns away from an uninterrupted sequence of golden tones, going for a chiffy, aspirated sound like that of a tracker-organ. At such points she often huffs out her extra air audibly before breathing, in a way that reinforces the strong beat in a phrase. In this way, she places her emphasis on rhythm above all, as Chris too stressed. At one point in our workshop, he declared that rhythm is "always at the top of the musical food-chain." He went so far as to say that if you miss notes, or even if your tone or your intonation is occasionally off, strong rhythm can still make your playing of Irish, Scottish, Cape Breton, and Québécois tunes engaging and effective.

Brad Hurley, who definitely focuses on the Irish idiom in his teaching rather than taking a pan-Celtic approach, nevertheless has his own ecumenical aspect in performance. His partner Claire Boucher is a native of Brittany whose traditional Breton singing fills their home just as his captivating Irish tunes on the flute do. Increasingly, they perform in concerts featuring both these Celtic traditions. In our era of increased mobility—when a Breton woman and a flute player who grew up in the Hudson Valley meet and make their home in Québec, when outstanding proponents of Irish flute playing like Catherine McEvoy regularly teach in summer workshops in the United States, France, and elsewhere, and when traditional Scottish musicians like the piper Hamish Moore come over to Cape Breton to rediscover the roots of their own national music and dance—we witness the dramatic spectacle of a Celtic swirl.

After becoming more serious about playing I sold the flute I had initially bought online and purchased, first, a keyless blackwood one and, several years later, a keyed flute in brown *mopane* wood. These latter two instruments were both made by Forbes and Yolanta Christie—a Scottish flute-maker and his Polish-American wife. An artisanal jeweler who went over to Scotland to hone her silver-smithing skills, Yolanta met and married Forbes there. After spending the first years of their marriage in Scotland and England, they came to Boston where Forbes worked as a master fabricator of silver flute-bodies in the celebrated Powell and Brannan companies before turning to simple-system wooden flutes, with Yolanta hand-forging, rather than casting, the keys. Their story exemplifies the same diaspora that traditional music also maps. Emigration and immigration, loss and recovery, contingency and confluence, tunes that turn into other tunes, that lose and reclaim their names, and that are discovered by a couple listening to them on an iPad beside a glowing stove in Vermont.

This diaspora represents both the dispersal of populations and the diffusion of a particular aesthetic. In the volume of *Connemara* entitled *A Little Gaelic Kingdom*, Tim Robinson compares the Celtic sense of beauty both to the replication of certain simple forms across different scales, as described in Benoît Mandelbrot's theory of fractals, and to the fabric of nature itself:

> Perhaps one could claim that fractal geometry is to Celtic art as Euclid is to classical art. While the main-stream of European culture has pursued its magnificent

course, another perception has been kept in mind by the Celtic periphery . . . in a word, that a fascinating sort of beauty arises out of the repetitive interweaving of simple elements. The beauty of nature is often of this sort. In Connemara, which is pre-eminently the land of 'dappled things'—drizzly skies, bubbly streams, tussocky hill-sides—one recognizes the texture.

This is a compelling way of to state the appeal of Irish music in particular, with its endless variations on elemental themes and its intricate margins along which shadowy melodies entwine with perky rhythms.

↜ I have picked up the flute at my own ragged edge, where I am neither entirely disentangled from my former reading and teaching nor settled confidently in the new habitat of retirement. I am an aging amateur exploring a zone far different from the realm of professional competence I came to take for granted over so many years. The stiffness of my right elbow when I stand to play the flute reminds me of the fact that I am physically winding down, just as the cut-over, boulder-strewn slope behind our house reminds me that I have left behind the expensive beauty of the Middlebury College campus. As I write this chapter, Rita, my partner in music as in everything else of greatest value, has been diagnosed with a neurological and genetically linked disorder that her brother in California has developed simultaneously. Because Rita's spinocerebellar ataxia (or SCA) is progressive it will color the rest of our marriage, becoming the drone that reverberates below every tune we play. Our tunes will need to rise up like ladders from this place of difficulty.

The Irish context of this memoir notwithstanding, I'm not thinking about ladders because of Yeat's "mound of refuse" at the end of "The Circus Animals' Desertion," with its indelible final lines, "now that my ladder's gone, / I must lie down where all the ladders start, / In the foul rag-and-bone shop of the heart." And if I am in fact thinking of our own poet Frost, it's not because of the way "After Apple-Picking" begins: "My old two-pointed ladder's sticking through a tree / Towards heaven still." Rather, I'm recollecting an exchange Frost once had with his friend Rabbi Victor Reichert. Despite the strong religious impulse so evident in his writing, the poet professed no orthodox belief of any kind. Still, he loved talking about the Bible and religion with Rabbi Reichert, who summered, as Frost did, in Ripton, near the Bread Loaf School of English. As I learned in reading *The Rabbi and the Poet* by Andrew Marks, Frost once asked his friend as they walked through the woods around Bread Loaf, "Victor, what do you think are the chances of life after death?" Reichert, good rabbi that he was, responded to this query with another question: "Robert, what do you think?" Frost's answer was, I believe, as close to a credo as he ever got: "With so many ladders going up everywhere, there must be *something* for them to lean against."

Hogback, retirement, and the hours I devote to a new instrument I'll never entirely master define the place my ladders start. Within this edge between the middle and the end my tunes rise up like aspirations, or like dreams. In *The Interpretation of Dreams* Freud introduces a concept akin to that of the ecotone, namely "the uncanny." People may appear recognizably in a dream but at the same time possess certain altered attributes, like hair-color, that connect them with others. Or symbolic features may be added to a dream's otherwise realistic surface, like, say, a stop-sign superimposed on the face of one's father. This mixture of the unfamiliar and the familiar is well expressed in the German word translated in English as "uncanny": *das Unheimliche*—which literally means the "unhomely." Such images give dreams their strangeness, and sometimes their humorousness, as well as make them feel mysteriously significant. Something is being conveyed but in an indirect, or even coded, fashion. Retirement feels like this to me, at once free and new and deeply retrospective. The Hogback Ridge does too, filled with rusty old logging chains and tumbled-down stone walls yet all the while growing ever wilder. As does "Langstrom Pony," toppling back and forth between A and G in ways that make my stomach drop then make me want to play it again.

Lucky Old Man

JERRY'S BEAVER HAT, *OR* THE YANK'S RETURN

As a recent immigrant to Irish music, and still a relative beginner when it comes to learning music by ear, I step into a new tune phrase by phrase and keep on the lookout for recognizable patterns. One noticeable aspect for me of the tunes I've been playing lately is that they just keep going up and down! While you could of course say the same for most other melodies, the jig "Jerry's Beaver Hat" has a bumptiousness about it that I find irresistible. It's a tune Rita and I learned during a session at Jonathan Leonard's house in Richmond, Vermont. The first measure bounds upward in an arpeggio from the D at the bottom of the flute's range to the one an octave above. The same brisk beginning also figures in other tunes like "Jackson's Morning Breeze," though in that case the tune skips even higher, to the G above the higher D. In "Jerry's Beaver Hat," however, the melody turns right around after the first measure and descends all the way back to the low opening note. After that comical up-and-down the register rises once more, before settling back down yet again, in a flutter of eight-note triplets, on the original D. Then, in the second part of the tune, the whole melody rises into a higher range than anything we've heard up to now. Rita homed in on how often there's a rise in the register between the A and B parts of many Irish tunes during our first summer at the Catskills Irish Arts Week. She was alert to it because the highest notes are over on the right-hand side of her concertina. In "Jerry's Beaver Hat," after a couple of go-rounds up there in the stratosphere around high B (which is effectively the top of the flute's range) down goes the tune again so that the vaulting exuberance of the opening can be repeated. Here's how it sounds.

The feeling that "Jerry's Beaver Hat" gives of skipping breathlessly up and down a dance floor has especially struck me because of the way it mirrors a certain bipolar aspect of my experience in retire-

LINK: *Jerry's Beaver Hat*

ment. Traveling to Ireland, learning to play the flute, and hiking around the woods above our home in the village of Bristol can all feel like aspects of a long, idyllic holiday. Though there will no longer be a fall semester curtailing what seems on many days to be a deliciously extended summer vacation, however, an end will come. I can feel it in my knees as I hike and in my fingers as I play. More to the point, as Rita's ataxia continues to progress slowly, both of us feel the preciousness of each day with a new poignancy. We've begun to explore options for a smaller, more accessible dwelling that will allow us to remain in Bristol if a move from our present house is necessary. But as Rita's mother used to say about her own aging process, "It's not as if anyone is singled out for this." In celebrating the satisfactions and discoveries of our days, as well as meeting the challenges that arrive, we seek to cultivate a spirit of equanimity.

In a workshop I attended with the flute god Kevin Crawford, before his concert at the Barre, Vermont Opera House with Martin Hayes and John Doyle, he recommended "throating" three repeated notes in the lower registers of a jig called "John McKenna's." This sharp, insistent *huh-huh-huh*, unadorned by cuts or other ornamentation, offered a strongly percussive alternative to the more graceful fluting in the upper reaches of a tune's second part. Throating is a more visceral and concussive alternative to the tonguing I learned on the French horn. It feels like a controlled and strategic chest-cough. The crisp breathiness with which Kevin accomplished this made me realize that this technique must also be how Catherine McEvoy achieves many of her own chiffy, percussive effects. When her tone rises into the upper register she often allows the phrasing to become more silvery and liquid again, producing a striking contrast within a single piece. Up and down, suave and rugged. That is the fascinating wholeness of such a style.

Such a contrast between musical modes within a single tune speaks not only to my experience in retirement but also to my shifting perspective on the pastoral literature that was my focus as a teacher at Middlebury. The topography described in this tradition typically lies along a ragged edge where the rocky soil is apparently better at germinating poems than at growing crops or sustaining rural economies. This is true in Wordsworth's Lake District, in the mountains of Frost's northern New England, as well as in Tim Robinson's books on the Aran Islands and Connemara—with their alertness to the continuing impact of the Great Hunger. In fact, Virgil's first Eclogue, the work that initiates and defines the pastoral tradition for me, is explicitly framed by a history of rural disruption and expropriation. In its central story of two aging smallholders challenged by changes in the larger world, this poem also speaks in a more pointed, and comical, way to my life as a flute player in Bristol. I never imagined Virgil would be pertinent to my relationship with the Irish flute. Yet here he is.

My mother Lois was a lover of Latin. The six children of her north Louisiana farm-family each supported the college education of the siblings immediately below them in age— both financially and in other ways. Her beloved older brother, my namesake Uncle John, transferred from Louisiana Tech to LSU when my mother was ready for college, since only in Baton Rouge could she pursue the Classics major she longed for. Three decades later, when I was a high-school student of Latin in Mill Valley, California, Mom and I would sit on the living room sofa while she went over my translations with me. Because she loved Virgil above all, so did I. I can remember, very clearly, reading the first five lines of Eclogue 1 with her, and getting a better sense through them of the graceful cadences of Latin verse.

Tityre, tu patulae recubans sub tegmine fagi
siluestrim tenui Musam meditaris auena;
nos patriae finis and dulcia linquimus arua.
nos patriam fugimus; tu, Tityre, lentus in umbra
formosam resonare doces Amaryllida siluas.

Here is Guy Lee's fairly literal translation of that opening, from the Penguin Classics paperback I liked to use with my students at Middlebury:

Tityrus, lying back beneath wide beechen cover,
You meditate the woodland Muse on slender oat;
We leave the boundaries and sweet ploughlands of home.
We flee our homeland; you, Tityrus, cool in shade,
Are teaching woods to echo Lovely Amaryllis.

I especially enjoyed, in those translation sessions with my mother, sorting out the crossword puzzle of the syntax. Since the verbs and nouns are both grammatically inflected, literary Latin has far less reliance than English on the basic subject-verb-object sentence order. Recalling this early taste of Virgil from my present standpoint as a student of Irish music, I can see that much of the pleasure in the trial-and-error process of translation, as in learning to play the flute by ear, came from the intense quality of awareness it lent to my beginner's mind. Moving so slowly through the first five lines, like learning each phrase of "Jerry's Beaver Hat" by rote, reinforced the passage's basic architecture. The tune's emphatic up-down, up-down has its poetic equivalent in Virgil's own symmetrical pattern of *tu-nos-nos-tu*, you-we-we-you, in the Eclogue's opening lines.

Even more than such musical patterns in Virgil's Latin verse, though, what brings the First Eclogue to mind now is its central conversation between two aging neighbors. A grizzled farmer named Meliboeus stumbles upon his old friend Tityrus, who is reclining in the shade and playing a love song on his pastoral pipes. In addressing him, Meliboeus goes back and forth between exclaiming about Tityrus's leisurely new circumstances and lamenting the dire changes in his own life. He seems astonished to find his friend, who has, until now, been a slave and thus far below the status of a freeholder like himself, lying back in the shade and "meditat[ing] the woodland Muse on a slender oat." Indeed, it feels as if Tityrus may have placed himself there beside the path specifically in order to flaunt his new freedom to the neighborhood. His posture, as described by the incredulous Meliboeus, distills the Classical ideal of *otium*, or sweet leisure, but in such an exaggerated fashion that it feels almost like a send-up. These lines, written by Virgil two thousand years ago, also mock a certain element of play-acting in my own life since retirement from Middlebury. Yet the image of Tityrus playing music as he reclines in the shade also expresses an enduring human desire for peaceful refuge from the heat of the day. Who doesn't sometimes long to escape from, or in some way to *elevate*, the effortfulness of our long-established routines? To listen for, and to perform, a music that might bring shape and consolation to our brief lives?

Lee translates the phrase *sub tegmine fagi* as "beneath wide beechen cover." One connotation of the word *tegmine* is that the branches and leaves of the beech function as a *roof* for him. As I know from visits to Rita's many relatives in a hill town east of Rome called Artena, Italians today still refer to each distinct space within a garden as a "stanza," or room. Such a way of speaking makes of the garden as a whole a delightful outdoor house. Tityrus, here, is *inhabiting* an experience of ease and beauty that was imagined in an unforgettable way by earlier poetry in Greek. As he plays the pipes while lolling about in such pleasant circumstances, he is adopting a studied and highly recognizable *pose*. Identifying himself, in fact, as the kind of poetic goat-herd whose mind is more absorbed by music and love than by plans for work. The reed pipe is thus an essential *trapping* for Tityrus in the new life he envisions for himself.

I can still remember, from that long-ago chapter of my life as a high-school student of Latin in Mill Valley, watching an episode of *The Smothers Brothers Comedy Hour* when they satirized a cowboy song that had been getting a lot of play on the radio. Part of their spoof of "The Streets of Laredo" went like this:

I see by your outfit that you are a cowboy.
I see by your outfit you are a cowboy too.
We see by our outfits that we are both cowboys.
If you get an outfit you can be a cowboy too.

My flute, like Tityrus's pipes, was part of the way I kitted myself out in retirement. For my own generation of Baby Boomers in America—so distant in other ways from Virgil's native Lombardy or Tityrus's imagined Arcadia—there seems to be a similar impulse for stage-managing our retirement as the start of a new life. Fly rods and mountain bikes, like my wooden flute, are emblems for the exciting new activities that will replace our workaday practices. Ways not just to amuse ourselves but also to develop new skills or hone our physical fitness now that there's finally sufficient space in our lives. These are purposeful sorts of hobbies, all the more so because in one's sixties there's inevitably an awareness, even with the advent of more spacious days, of being in a race against time.

One of the reasons satire has always been so central to the pastoral tradition, as well as to critiques of it, is that leisure enjoyed amid beautiful landscapes does nothing to stop the clock. In the seventeenth-century reimaginings of the pastoral by painters like Poussin, those misty rural scenes are brought into sharp relief by rustics' discovery of a partially obscured gravestone or by the white gleam of a skull within the shady woods. *Et in Arcadia ego*, "I too am in Arcadia," such images of mortality confide. There's bound to be something comical about the moment when we self-anointed swains catch an echo of this voice. What, after all, might one have expected? A cartoon on the door of the Bristol Fitness Center, where members of our generational cohort strive each morning to account preemptively for the coming evening's calories, shows two women jogging together down a leafy street. One glances over to the other, saying, "I'm thinking about just letting myself get old."

Pastoral satire is more than cynicism, however. The fantasies of rejuvenation and of personal security in a turbulent world always collide with time and history in the end. But the collapse of such illusions can also be an opening door—a way to rejoin the topsy-turvy world truly inhabited by others. If mortality calls the question for our various self-improving projects in retirement, the turmoil and inequity within our own communities do the same for the idyllic landscapes in which we had imagined pursuing our various enthusiasms. This world of reverses and instability is the context, and in some sense the subject, of the dialogue that follows from Meliboeus's first sighting of the would-be swain.

Tityrus responds to his neighbor's questions by explaining that he traveled down to Rome in order to apply for release from his servile status. The"god" who granted his petition is generally identified as the young Octavian, destined to become Augustus. Liberty came late for Tityrus, though, "after my beard fell whiter to the barber's trim." It also arrived just when Meliboeus and many of their other neighbors were having their lands expropriated. Veterans of the victorious armies at Philippi were granted farms safely distant from the capital, and tradition has it that Virgil's family even had their own lands near Mantua confiscated at this time. Interspersed with Tityrus's descriptions of his providential trip to Rome is thus Meliboeus's account of losing everything at the hands of the same divinely remote and powerful figures who liberated Tityrus.

After hearing of Tityrus's favored treatment by "a god," Meliboeus replies:

> *I am not envious, more amazed: the countryside's*
> *All in such turmoil. Sick myself, look, Tityrus,*
> *I drive goats forward; this one I can hardly lead.*
> *For here in the hazel thicket just now dropping twins,*
> *Ah, the flock's hope, on naked flint, she abandoned them.*

To be thrust off his land, for a farmer like Meliboeus who has known no other home or employment, is to lose past, present, and future in one catastrophe. He pictures his fellow exiles and himself fanning out on inhospitable paths that will lead them into unknown lands of an empire stretching from Africa to Britain. Meanwhile, "Some godless veteran will own this fallow tilth, / Those cornfields a barbarian." Here, he addresses at once the historical reality that many of Caesar's returning veterans were not Italians and the fact that Tityrus himself will now be living in a disrupted and barely recognizable neighborhood.

"Amazed" as he is, both by the devastation visited on him by distant power-brokers and by Tityrus's unexpected reversal of fortune, it's startling that Meliboeus can still pause and express an interest in his friend's new life. In a passage that's become central to my own understanding of retirement, he sums up Tityrus's altered situation in a beautiful, if tonally complex, benediction:

> *Lucky old man, the land then will remain your own,*
> *And large enough for you, although bare rock and bog*
> *With muddy rushes covers all the pasturage:*
> *No unaccustomed feed will try your breeding ewes,*
> *And no infection harm them from a neighbor's flock.*
> *Lucky old man, among familiar rivers here*
> *And sacred springs you'll angle for the cooling shade . . .*

The repeated words "Lucky old man" are translated as "Happy old man" in the Loeb Classical Library's prose version of the Eclogue. But I prefer Guy Lee's choice, and not only because the Latin is "Fortunaté senex," rather than "Felix senex" as that alternative would imply. "Lucky" also reinforces the fact that Tityrus's happiness, like the suffering of Meliboeus and others in the neighborhood, is contingent upon the whim of detached "gods." Along with the Eclogue's opening five lines and Tityrus's five lines that will conclude the Eclogue, this speech is, for me, one of the poem's defining passages. As is so often true both in Virgil and in Ireland's modal tunes, the essential meaning of his passage is carried by its haunting *tone*. Meliboeus's emphasis is not on any achievement or virtue on Tityrus's part, but simply on the surprising, if favorable, nature of his situation in contrast with Meliboeus's own.

Even if compared with my earlier explorations of Irish music and retirement, western Ireland and the Green Mountains, as variations on a theme, the present excursion into Virgil may feel like quite a stretch! The fact is, though, that it speaks directly to my increasing awareness of *myself* as a lucky old man. It's not only that for several years now I have had the luxury of days filled with music and seasons enriched by travel. "Lucky," as opposed to "happy," also registers the tenuousness of this fortunate moment. Rita and I too have heard from behind a beech tree (or in our case behind a sugar maple) a voice whispering "Et in Arcadia ego." This chapter of our lives is not less precious for being transitory. But remembering its contingency, and its inevitable brevity, may also help us become more attuned to broader social and personal narratives. I would describe neither Middlebury College nor TIAA-CREF, the organization that administers my retired professor's annuity, as godlike. Yet these hefty institutions are the equivalent of Tityrus's Roman sponsors, in making possible, at least for now, long afternoons of *otium*. Many others, in America and abroad as well as right here in our village of Bristol, have not been lucky enough to receive such support.

⤸ Like the yawing up and down of "Jerry's Beaver Hat," Meliboeus's speech begins with stark reversals between wonder and complaint. But then his tone begins to hover reflectively over the rugged pastoral edge where Tityrus's existence will now be mapped. "[T]he land then will remain your own, / And large enough for you" are lines that reflect this opening oscillation. The fact that Meliboeus no longer possesses his *own* land sums up the catastrophe shadowing his life—just at the moment when ownership has finally come to Tityrus after a lifetime in which he didn't even have legal title to his own labor. "[L]arge enough for you" expresses with precision the scanty sufficiency of Tityrus's new holding. Because he is a "senex" with no family, a small flock, and few needs, this scrap of land where rock and reeds crowd out the pasture will just about serve for him. Those returning veterans have been given the fatter soil and broader fields previously owned by farmers like Meliboeus. Though they may be "godless" in the sense of not being Italians attuned to the traditional deities of this place, they are in fact much more favored than even Tityrus by the political pantheon surrounding Octavian in Rome.

In its totality, however, Meliboeus's speech also evokes the benefits of Tityrus's marginal smallholding and affirms the apparent contradictions that have defined pastoral poetry ever since. In this way it also once more recalls the concept of ecotones. Virgil's First Eclogue emphatically locates Tityrus, his aging and initially clueless swain, along just such an edge. Meliboeus describes his neighbor's marginal new property most strikingly by noting its characteristic sounds:

The hedge this side, along your neighbour's boundary,
Its willow flowers as ever feeding Hybla bees,
Will often whisper you persuasively to sleep;
The pruner under that high bluff will sing to the breeze,
Nor yet meanwhile will cooing pigeons, your own brood,
Nor turtledove be slow to moan from the airy elm.

Tityrus's new land lies between the readily cultivatable land of more prosperous farmers and the uncultivated woods. It is bounded by a hedge along the downhill border while thick woods rise on the slope above him. Because of this transitional zone's narrowness it partakes of the beauty of both adjacent realms, with the bees "whispering" to Tityrus from the willow hedge, a pruner singing from farther below "that high bluff," his own pigeons cooing around him, and turtledoves calling from the trees that rise above. The essential crop of his new land is music, in short—harmonies of the edge. The reference to Hybla bees makes the music of this pastoral edge a sort of honey, sweetening a world of reversals such as the speaker Meliboeus has himself suffered. Within this passage I recognize the way in which music has also become the honey of this new edge of Rita's and my life too.

With its mysterious power of consolation, music may be *harvested* along this ragged edge where bees buzz in the hedges and flowers bloom uncultivated by human hands. Likewise, a capacity for sympathy and identification with others may germinate at such a boundary. From this point on in the Eclogue Tityrus's own tone also changes. Self-absorption and complacency give way to compassion for his neighbors' losses, and to an impulse toward generosity in the use of his own, though paltry, new resources. One way to think of Tityrus's pastoral ecotone, situated as it is at an edge between cultivated lands and the woods, would be as the selvage completing a piece of fabric. In our lives too such loosely woven boundaries offer not only scenes of unraveling but opportunities for something new to happen. Empathy, like music, can grow at such an edge.

↪ "Jerry's Beaver Hat" has an alternative title: "The Yank's Return." Given the often whimsical nature of titles in Irish music, as Ciaran Carson discusses in his book *Last Night's Joy*, one needs to be careful about connecting the title of a given tune too closely to its meaning. Having said that, though, I still can't resist combining these two titles into a narrative related to the jaunty jig they name. In one such possible version Jerry may be a returning emigrant who ostentatiously sports a beaver hat as a sign of his increased prosperity. It's as hard (read: impossible) for a flourishing former neighbor to avoid obnoxiousness when coming back around to display his success as it would be, say, for a retiree from Middlebury College to call up former colleagues in the midst of their end-of-term grading and tell them all about a recent snorkeling holiday. Our various forms of new hats inevitably become the focus of both annoyance and mockery.

Beaver hats in particular, though substantial and expensive, would no longer have been the height of fashion for very long after the flood of Irish emigration that began in the 1840s. In addition to hearing about ecotones from my ecologist colleagues at Middlebury, I learned from them that beavers had come perilously close to extinction in North America because of centuries of unremitting demand for beaver hats in European and American cities. An unexpected consequence of the silk top hat's growing preeminence in the mid-nineteenth-century was that demand for beaver pelts plummeted and these little engineers could re-establish themselves on northern waterways. Lucky old beavers! But this evolution in haberdashery might also have meant that Jerry looked simultaneously ostentatious and silly in his expensive beaver hat—a foolish oldster sporting the style of a bygone era.

☞ Playing his oaten pipes in the shade while neighbors straggled by with their disoriented flocks was Tityrus's version of a beaver hat. I can see now that my own pleasure in playing the flute on the sun-warmed porch of our North Street house may have sometimes been my own equivalent. I didn't *think* of this as making a display, but as neighbors walked by on the sidewalks or cruised by in their cars they may have been at least as aware of me as I was of them. The noticeability of my playing music as others were probably going to or getting out of work reinforced a broader contrast. A number of Bristol's residents were born in and still inhabit comfortable old houses like the one we had lived in on North Street for the better part of four decades. Often they have either inherited their homes or purchased them from relatives or friends so that they could continue to lead a rewarding life within their extended families while employed in the local lumbermills and stores. In recent years, though, more and more local residents have needed to commute to Middlebury, Vergennes, or Burlington in order to support their households in Bristol. As property values soared, the prospects for Bristolites in our children's generation to live here drastically diminished. Even the recession of 2008 did not reset the cost of local homes to anything near what it was when Rita and I came to town. Meanwhile, many people like ourselves "from away" have been drawn to Bristol's leafy streets and the dramatic beauty of its setting in the mountains.

Beyond such economic disparities, certain differences in outlooks between old-timers and newcomers like us can also lead to mutual incomprehension or, at times, to conflict in the community. Rita and I have always preferred living in Bristol to life in Middlebury precisely because of the relative absence of fancy shops and expensive cars here. It's a working-class town whose schools, municipal governance, churches, and other local organizations have just felt more comfortable for us. The fact remains, though, that because I was a college teacher with a retirement fund shepherded by TIAA-CREF and growing over the years with the help of Middlebury College's monthly matches, we were able to remain securely in the house we loved. Many people who were here when we arrived are finding it more and more difficult now to pay their taxes and heat their homes.

Municipal planning, for a deeply rooted rural town like

Bristol, is a process in which the dissonance between natives and immigrants can really jangle. Those whose families have so long been rooted here can view their new neighbors as "godless veterans," oblivious to the character and traditions of the town, and insensitive about piling new taxes onto an already burdened citizenry. Later arrivals, for their part, can sometimes suspect those who were already in town of not being alert enough to national and global developments that threaten the future of a vulnerable community like Bristol. In an earlier chapter I compared Bristol and Roundstone from the vantage-points of the Hogback Ridge and Mt. Errisbeg. I still frequently clear my head by walking out our backdoor and up onto the Ledges above our village. But when Rita and I take our evening walk with Shadow now, in order to settle our dinner before playing some tunes in the living room, we generally head off in the opposite direction. We cross the core of the village, skirt the Bristol landfill, then circle the playing fields of Mount Abraham Union High School.

Our daughter Rachel and sons Matthew and Caleb all attended this sprawling two-story structure of brick and stone. Whenever walking around it I thus also swim through memories of parent-teacher conferences, craft fairs, band concerts, musicals, and soccer games, like so many pockets of warm water in a lake. There and gone. An oversteepened precipice just west of the school marks the boundary of an adjacent gravel pit whose hummocky surface lies a hundred feet below. After several decades of extraction, this site is pretty well played out. But active gravel quarries are still in operation not too far to the north and south of the high school. As I write this chapter, a proposal for another nearby operation has been at the center of a toxic controversy in our town for more than a decade.

In my capacity as a member of Bristol's Planning Commission I've recently participated in a series of televised hearings aiming to sort out the results of questionnaires we distributed to our fellow citizens. They solicited Bristolites' opinions about where extraction should be permitted and under what restrictions. Respondents at one end of the spectrum expressed outrage that we would even consider allowing the noise and dirt of a new gravel pit anywhere near the historical center of the village, while a worried middle ground of residents longed for a way to balance environmental concerns with our sagging economy's need for stimulus as well as for the large amounts of gravel required on our roads and in new construction. At the other extreme were supporters of unfettered property-rights who objected to the very existence of a Select Board-appointed Planning Commission. One such respondent wrote on the green form passed out in Holley Hall, "Who the fuck do you people think you are?" Good question.

⌐ Reading Robinson's books on Connemara helped me to draw connections between the geological histories of western Ireland and Vermont at the level of bedrock. But fully as influential on both regions' current prospects as their tectonic DNA is the subsequent and also shared story of glaciation between about 20,000 and 12,000 years ago. Looking west from where the mowed strip behind Mt. Abe High School suddenly drops away we can see the shining ribbon of Lake Champlain. Fort

Ticonderoga lies directly across from us on the New York side, with its restored battlements and stockades, where each summer there are reenactments of the outdoor military exercises known as tattoos that recall one vivid chapter in this region's history. But the gravel deposits immediately below my feet record another one.

They mark the shore of prehistoric Lake Vermont, whose waters once extended twenty-one miles east of Lake Champlain's present edge and lapped against the grassy edge where my feet are now planted. A few miles north of here they found valleys through which they could extend as far east as Montpelier and Barre, while here in Addison County Snake Mountain was transformed into an island. Lake Vermont was a post-glacial phenomenon. The Wisconsin Glaciation had compressed this part of North America under a mile of ice, grinding down what had been a Himalaya-high extension of the Appalachian chain into the rounded Green Mountains we know today. After the ice finally began to melt the land sprang back up with the release of that colossal weight in a "glacial rebound" that progressed from south to north.

This post-glacial tilting of the land explains why so many of our main rivers in western Vermont—like Otter Creek, Addison County's "Indian Highway"—flow north. For Lake Champlain too, though it might seem on a map to dwindle away and vanish to the *south*, north was in fact the new downhill. When an ice-plug in the Richelieu River corked that outflow the ancient Lake Vermont was created, widening until it finally reached the shore established by a line of thrust-faults near what are now upland towns like Bristol. Meanwhile, though, the oceans were also rising, as less and less of the earth's water was locked up in ice. Saltwater accordingly rushed down into Lake Vermont, reversing the direction of the Saint Lawrence and the Richelieu and creating a marine phenomenon geologists now describe as the Champlain Sea.

More melting and more ice plugs brought a second freshwater Lake Vermont, replaced in its turn by a second Champlain Sea. During these dramatic periods of inundation and reversal heavy siltation laid down the nutrient-rich clay subsoils of the Champlain Valley, one of New England's most productive agricultural regions. An inkling of this dramatic sequence came in 1849, when a farmer in nearby Charlotte gazed in astonishment at the whale skeleton unearthed from one of his fields by a crew excavating for a railroad cut. It was a bewildering relic of those melted glaciers and evaporated seas.

The high plateau on which the village of Bristol stands, and the necklace of sandpits and gravel quarries strung along its edge, are also relics. The flat terrain supporting our compact grid of streets originated as the broad fan of a delta. The roomy clapboard houses of North Street are planted on the well-drained soils where an unruly ancestor of today's New Haven River once poured through Bristol Gap, slowing as it debouched into Lake Vermont. Gravel and sand that had been swept along by strong currents sank when water met water, laying down the deposits that we mine today. The heavy Vergennes clays disked and harrowed by farmers to the west of Bristol with their behemoth green (John Deere), orange (Kubota), and blue (New Holland) tractors testify to an earlier world in which whales swam high above the present level of their unsuspecting, feed-capped heads. Up here in our community at the ancient shore, the controversy over extraction that continues to divide our town and muddy our civic harmony was sown into the soil as gravel. I wonder when we'll finish digging it out, like so many dragons' teeth. Meanwhile, though I had anticipated floating off to new adventures, I too have settled at this gravelly shore, my threshold.

There's clearly something ludicrous about Tityrus, piping in the shade, Jerry the returning Yank sporting his beaver hat, and for that matter me, in my faded jeans, picking up the flute. But while these gestures are, from one perspective, half-baked, they also offer moments when a conversation can start. Meliboeus can't help stepping over to find out what's going on under the shade of that beech tree. In doing so he launches a dialogue through which Tityrus in turn comes to see that the countryside has been enveloped in a catastrophe, with his own good fortune merely a ripple at the margin. In *Connemara*, when investigating evidences of suffering and dislocation from the latter half of the nineteenth-century, Robinson surveys the ruins scattered across a depopulated landscape and observes that the Great Hunger is still not over. Such a hugely wounding fact will linger on for centuries, shadowing every subsequent choice amid the rocky beauty of that peninsula with the ache of absence.

New accounts have noted that carbon in the atmosphere has surpassed 400 parts per million, with 350 having been established several years ago by James Hansen at NASA as the line after which climate stability will be impaired. Our winters are already notably shorter in Vermont, our summers rainy enough to be increasingly marked by floods. Though we continue to plant our gardens, talk on the telephone with our children, and enjoy our dinners, climate change is already here, just as the Great Hunger still casts its shadow across Ireland today. Such anticipated and remembered disasters absorb our individual projects and challenges into the vaster dramas of our landscape and community. The occasional silliness or neediness of strategies for shoring up our shifting lives, along with their accompanying trappings, subside into a more sober conversation about where we all might need to head next.

꙳ As so much is swept away, though, music remains, both as an expression of the earth's beauty and as an experience of collective memory. After visiting a friend in Galway Rita and I once ventured up into County Mayo. Our base of operations was the lovely town of Westport, where a particular attraction was Matt Molloy's Pub. Molloy was a glamorous figure for me, as the flute player for the Chieftains in their heyday and a performer who redefined the possibilities of his instrument. On the evening when we dropped by that establishment neither he nor any of his celebrated musical friends were playing. But there was nonetheless an appealing little session in the backroom. As in many pubs we visited, this was less an open and informal gathering of musicians than a handful of local stalwarts who had presumably been paid a bit, or at least given free drinks, to play for us tourists. The music was lively and enjoyable, led by an excellent fiddle player and also featuring a button accordion, a bodhran, and a guitar.

As in Clare, the tempos here were not too fast and the musicians were enjoying their pints along with the two dozen or so of us seated at battered oak tables in an unpretentious space between the main bar and the privies out back. After every few sets, the leader would call on a white-haired gentleman seated against the wall for a story or a song. "No, I don't know anything," he'd reply with a grumpy air, but after a bit more cajoling he'd always relent and sing. This little drama played out several times as we sat there, and in each case the first thing the singer did was to ask someone in the audience where they were from. It turned out, on this gray winter day, that they were all from Ireland: Limerick, Cork, Dublin.

Each of the songs he sang was in the voice of an Irish emigrant forced to leave behind one of the towns our fellow tourists hailed from. These laments from across the sea recalled the exiles' loving family and friends in Ireland, never to be seen again, and also celebrated the beauty of the seasons and landscape that had surrounded them in childhood. Even though the verses may at some points have felt formulaic, the reality of a permanent sundering of deep human connections provided a sobering counter-balance to such sentimental touches. These songs had traveled exactly as far—though in the opposite direction—as the emigrants who had earlier departed. They were now being performed, and listened to, by those who'd never left. For the present-day singer and his listeners, sympathy rose to the intensity of personal identification. Music, like grieving, was the vehicle for both haunting and reunion. These remarkable experiences of tidal departure and return linger in my ear as an unending rhythm of confluence. In retiring, in settling down to do the gravelly work of community, and in picking up the flute, I too must give myself over to a lyrical world of striving, loss, and persistence.

Shadows and Apples

THE MONTH OF JANUARY

I STARE INTO THE MURKY IMAGE ON MY iPad as if something glimpsed there might bring "The Month of January" into sharper resolution. Nicholas Williams taught me this mysterious slow air when he stopped by Rita's and my cabin in Craftsbury, Vermont shortly before Christmas one year for a flute lesson. I had met Nicholas a couple of weeks earlier when Crowfoot, a guitar, fiddle, and flute trio specializing in Celtic and Québécois music, gave a concert at Rokeby. This is a nineteenth-century farm and Underground Railway station to the north of Bristol that now functions as a folk-life museum. Admiring Nicholas's musicianship and not having a teacher of the wooden flute living nearby, I emailed after the concert to ask if he would be willing to give me some instruction next time he was traveling through Vermont from his home in the Eastern Townships of Québec. It turned out that Crowfoot was just about to play for a contra dance at Sterling College in Craftsbury.

Our cabin is off the grid and I had neglected to bring my nifty little Edirol recorder for this lesson. When Nicholas noticed that I was typing some notes about the lesson into an iPad he pointed out that I could also use its camera function to record the pieces he would be teaching me. Thus I came out of the session with videos as well as audios of these new tunes. Not only was this late-afternoon lesson occurring in northern Vermont during the approach to Solstice, it was also taking place in a room whose walls were composed of gray cedar logs, with candles as the only illumination. So Nicholas and his flute appear on the screen as an indistinct shape pulsing to the tunes—except for a few moments when one of the silver keys on his blackwood instrument gleams in the candle light. As I gaze into those dark images now it feels almost like closing my eyes to concentrate on a haunting and recessive piece of music.

Even as Rita and I have thrown ourselves into playing Irish music over the past several years, we have steered away from the slow airs. Dance tunes lock into a solid rhythm. If you find the right tempo for a particular tune it takes on a swing that can help dancers move through their steps with confidence and grace. And when the two of us play by the woodstove in our Bristol living room, a danceable tempo adds to our melodies the propulsive echo of dancing feet.

By contrast, performances of slow airs can be expressive and irregular to an extreme, with measures prolonged or broken off according to the original words' emotional content. Taps, cuts, rolls, and other normally brisk forms of articulation can be stretched out, so that they begin to function as melodic elements in their own right rather than simply ways of dividing the notes in a line. When played rather than sung, a heartfelt and dramatic interpretation still remains essential to slow airs—though this can obviously be a special challenge to instrumentalists who don't know Irish when a particular air is in that language. Fortunately for me, "The Month of January" is sung in English, and available on one of our CDs in a powerful recording by Sinéad Cahir. Nevertheless this lament, in the voice of a young unwed mother with an infant in her arms who has been expelled from her parents' home in the depth of winter, continues to challenge me on an emotional level with its bleak remoteness.

One of the hardest parts for me to memorize from Nicholas's iPad version, and also among the most affecting, was his treatment of the song's very beginning: "It was in the month of January. / The hills were clad in snow." He ornaments the notes corresponding to "in" and "month" in such a slow and irregular fashion that I couldn't easily relate them to familiar rhythmic patterns even after listening to the recording over and over. A distraught and abandoned feeling is established in the opening phrases by this immediate faltering in the rhythm, as well as by a proliferation of cutting and sliding notes that undermine any sense of dwelling securely in a given mode or melody. Foreboding suffuses this slow disassembly of the air's first eight beats, even though the accompanying words' initial two *sentences*, to which those notes correspond, do nothing more than indicate the season. After two intervening musical lines, also of eight beats each, the tune's distraught opening is repeated from beginning to end. By that point in the lyrics themselves the main subject has finally been introduced:

the lamentation by "a pretty fair maid" who "had a baby in her arms / And bitter she did cry." As her story continues to unscroll in the air, the music accompanying each new stanza begins and closes with the same weird simplicity that framed the opening one.

LINK: *The Month of January*

This air was included in my lesson because I had asked for help with the distinctive vibrato that is produced on the Irish flute not from the diaphragm but rather by the player's fingertips rapidly wavering above certain open holes on the flute. The first two notes on which Nicholas produced this effect in his own playing of "The Month of January" were the ones corresponding to "hills" and "snow." The throbbing effect reinforced the tone of lamentation already established by the elaborate cuts and also prepared for the coming story of cruelty and suffering. The expressive impact of this effect was reinforced when the same musical phrase repeated at the end of the stanza—with the vibrato alighting this time on the second syllable of "bitter" and the final word "cry."

The voice of this young mother facing a homeless northern winter with her baby spoke to my own feelings of dread in approaching the darkest season of my third year since retirement. When I finally got back up into the mountains after recovering from polymyalgia, the evidence of climate change in Vermont's woods was devastating. Winters have become on average a month shorter since Rita and I moved to Vermont in 1973. The onset of sugaring season—so important to our sense of place—has become erratic and unpredictable, with extreme variations of thawing and freezing that threaten the germination of future generations of sugar maples. When I venture out later in the spring to see the woodland wildflowers, too, I now know from recent experience that there will be evidence everywhere of invasives from warmer regions, like knotweed, buckthorn, honeysuckle, and garlic mustard, each of them challenging the stability and health of our forests.

In the midst of such daunting changes, playing music daily with Rita has become an even more important experience of discovery and escape, a realm for exploration in which our musical technique and repertoire continued to improve at a satisfying pace. But even as Rita's playing soared, the onset of her ataxia clouded our future prospects for more long walks together. Our idyllic hopes for this epoch of our marriage amid the beauty of Vermont were staggered by these distinct but simultaneous developments. My sense of identification with Tityrus, which had initially been sparked by his delight in piping under the shade of that beech tree, was deepened now by the connection between his sober realizations in the course of the Eclogue and the new realities confronting both Vermont and our marriage. The final line of that poem brought me the same shudder of recognition that I now found in the quavering vibrato of "The Month of January": "*maioresque cadunt altis de montibus umbrae,*" "And down from the high mountains taller shadows fall."

When I taught seminars on the pastoral at Middlebury I often divided our initial session between the first Eclogue and the 23rd Psalm. Virgil's progression from pastoral shade to mortal shadows was anticipated by the Psalmist David at a decisive turning in his own poem: "Yea, though I walk through the valley of the shadow of death, I will fear no evil." Before that line the speaker praises God in the third-person: "The Lord is my shepherd. I shall not want." After experiencing the mountains' terrifying darkness, though, he switches to a more fervid and personal intimacy: *I will fear no evil: for thou art with me; thy rod and thy staff they comfort me.* Just as the process of learning Irish music has led me to reinhabit and reconsider my life of reading and teaching at the college, so too it takes me back to the beginning of my own literary and religious experience. Before I ever sat on the sofa parsing Virgil with her, my mother was also the one who introduced me to the 23rd Psalm.

My parents were devout Southern Baptists and reading the Bible together at meals as well as at church was central to our family as I was growing up. My early fascination with those shadowy stories and their lofty and mysterious King James English strongly influenced my eventual decision to study literature in college, as well as my path as a teacher and writer. Dad, my brother Lyn, and I all owned beautiful copies of the Bible, printed by Cambridge University Press on India-paper and bound in black Morocco leather. My two most glamorous possessions as a boy were this stately volume and my supple Richie Ashburn-model fielder's mitt. Mom had a lovely leather binding on her Bible, too, but chose to order it in her favorite color of sky blue. I've never seen another Bible of just that color. Its abiding association for me (beyond the fact that it matched both my mother's eyes and the woodwork in our Mill Valley kitchen) is with the tender blues and greens of a vernal landscape photograph that hung on the wall beside my bed when I was a child. Superimposed on this image were the kindly countenance of Jesus and the text of Psalm 23.

This Psalm was the first poem I ever memorized, learning it line by line from my mother Lois before I could read. The comforting cadences of the Shepherd David, like the goodness and mercy of my parents, have followed me all the days of my life. Just as, from the time of Plato, lovers of music have identified certain intervals and keys with particular colors, the language of the 23rd Psalm remains inseparable for me from the green of that long-lost photograph's pastures and the blue of its still waters. Another personal association of this poem is with my mother's cool hand (fragrant with the almond-scent of Jergens Lotion), resting on my forehead as she tried to help one young dervish stop spinning at the end of the day.

As the 23rd Psalm arrives at its last two verses there is another shift of voice. The speaker has gone from identifying himself as a sheep protected by a skilled shepherd to being an honored guest in the house of God:

Thou preparest a table before me in the presence of mine enemies: thou anointest my head with oil; my cup runneth over.
Surely goodness and mercy shall follow me all the days of my life: and I will dwell in the house of the Lord for ever.

Even as a boy I felt the musical satisfaction of this emphatic closing. Repeating it prepared me for the grand, thumping reiterations of Beethoven when I got to play the horn in performances of his third, fifth, and ninth symphonies later in life. Returning to these lines as a college teacher I could also admire the artfulness of that second-to-last verse. In contrast to the doublings which characteristically lend structure to lines of Hebrew poetry, when the cup runs over so does this verse of the Psalm—enumerating yet a *third* element of God's goodness that makes the poetry too brim and spill.

I also experienced a sense of tension at that overflowing and affirmative moment in Psalm, though. How was I, so closely identified by now with the speaker, supposed to feel about "the presence of mine enemies"? The very fact that I might actually *have* enemies disturbed me, as a boy growing up in a protective and kindly family. These strangers' looming "presence" sounded more purposeful and malicious than the dangers of the high mountain pass through which the speaker was shepherded earlier. Even if such antagonists did exist somewhere in the world, why did they have to be invited right into the divine mansions to stare as I took my place at the table? I would have enjoyed my new role as a divinely favored denizen of heaven much more without such unfriendly faces in the immediate field of vision. On the other hand, I felt that even if all the enemies were in fact deleted from that scene, I would have liked *someone* else there to help me enjoy this celebration after a hard journey. My family perhaps? Surely I hadn't been the only sheep guided through that dark valley. That would have been a pretty lonely excuse for a flock.

The dissonance in this memory of a great religious poem bears both on my engagement with Irish music now and on my earlier pleasure at Middlebury College in facilitating conversations among my students. My goal was for the students to experience how their voices could authentically converge, as interpretations accrued depth and complexity beyond the capacities of any of us individual readers. Given my love for *To the Lighthouse*, I came to view each book or poem on the syllabus as a table at which our seminar could gather. Just as a given discussion could be valuable in leading us toward a fuller appreciation of a great work of art, so too consideration of each work of literature could enrich our conversation and foster our growth into a true intellectual community.

Returning to both poems at this challenging moment in retirement, I feel more strongly than ever how directly the Psalm anticipates that Eclogue written a thousand years after it. Though the longing to find a place of safety, in the face of history and mortality alike, remains a deeply human one, the images of the favored guest at the Psalm's end and of the rejuvenated swain at the beginning of the Eclogue feel at once complex, instable, and close to home. An initial aspect of retirement for me was stepping exuberantly outside my institutional responsibilities and professional identity. But severing such ties can also feel like a freefall. When after the first moment of liberation others step *into* view, as Meliboeus did for Tityrus with his story of loss, they inevitably introduce tension. At the same time, such previously unaccounted for "presences" beside the table of solitude can offer a necessary escape from isolation. The dissonance of "enemies," as of all the other counter-narratives impinging on our idyllic expectations, can only be resolved through their integration into a more inclusive vision of landscape and community.

Tityrus's outlook changes after he listens to his old friend's tale of loss. But the old farmer Meliboeus's own perspective and voice also shift by the time of his final speech in the Eclogue. After those understandably bitter allusions to the "godless veteran" and the "barbarian" who will be taking over his pastures, cornfields, pear trees, and vineyards, he turns to address his livestock in a turning as decisive as the speaker's in Psalm 23. He had earlier imagined the animals and himself making their way to new lands together, under circumstances of great difficulty. Now, however, he *relinquishes* the flock, allowing it to remain among familiar fields even though he must now depart.

> *Go, little she-goats, go, once happy flock of mine.*
> *Not I hereafter, stretched full length in some green cave,*
> *Shall watch you far off hanging on a thorny crag;*
> *I'll sing no songs; not in my keeping, little goats,*
> *You'll crop the flowering Lucerne and bitter willow.*

What makes this speech more than an expression of loss is Meliboeus's own complex act of identification; first with his goats and then with the newly liberated Tityrus. While they are no longer *his* happy flock, the animals will nonetheless be able to remain in a landscape whose forage and sources of water they know. While "lucky," or *fortunaté*, earlier described Tityrus's unexpected change of circumstance, "happy," or *felix*, is now the word Meliboeus applies to these goats remaining in their home and thus exempt from the burden of emigration to unknown dangers in Africa and Britain. As he depicts his own former happiness, gazing at his flock feeding among the heights while "stretched full length in some green cave," Meliboeus also imagines himself in a posture of *otium* strikingly like the one in which he found Tityrus at the Eclogue's beginning. All he would need to reinforce the parallel would be some pastoral pipes—or maybe even a wooden Irish flute.

Meliboeus's generosity in envisioning abundance and health within a landscape from which he has been expelled by those distant Roman "gods" fosters a more imaginative and generous spirit in Tityrus too. Rather than stretching back out beneath the shade of the beech with his oaten pipes, he now turns toward his unfortunate neighbor with a timid though heartfelt invitation:

> *However, for tonight you could rest here with me*
> *Upon green leafage: I can offer you ripe fruit*
> *And mealy chestnuts and abundance of milk cheese.*
> *Far off the roof-tops of the farms already smoke*
> *And down from the high mountains taller shadows fall.*

The modesty of this invitation makes it feel especially touching and genuine. Tityrus can only offer a night of respite rather than any more lasting improvement of Meliboeus's lot. The tentativeness of the first verb *poteras*, which the Loeb version translates literally as "you might have" rested, conveys the timidity, and also the delicacy, of his invitation. I also prefer the specificity of the Loeb's "ripe apples," rather than Guy Lee's more strictly accurate "ripe fruit" for *poma*. Apples are the local fruit, in Ireland, Italy, and Vermont alike, that can be stored through the winter with careful management. Tityrus's initial song of himself, to the tune of

"Sweet Amaryllis," gives way here to a chastened and compassionate mode of hospitality. The artificiality with which he sought to represent his newly happy state at the beginning falls away, and he inhabits a more authentic, three-dimensional identity as he invites his neighbor to the table under those lengthening shadows.

⌖ Rita's and my anxiety about the progression of her ataxia increased the sense of dread that had been growing in me because of the change in Vermont's maple forests. I can see now that throwing myself into our family's sugarmaking endeavor a dozen years earlier had been, on one level, a precursor to my fascination with the Irish flute. As I bustled around the steamy sugarhouse in a retro red-and-black plaid jacket from Johnson Woolens, I was also trying out an alternative identity, and get-up, from my usual mode as a college professor. But the Arcadian simplicity I glimpsed in this traditional Vermont lifeway was challenged by fundamental changes to sugar-maple regeneration in the Green Mountains. Maple seeds germinate at thirty-four degrees, colder than any other native hardwood. As germination begins to happen more often during January's increasingly extended thaws, however, it may still be followed by more cold weather and heavy snows in February or March, resulting in the loss of many seedlings. Where I had looked hopefully to a long-established, stable practice, and where I had taken delight in a traditional, seasonally inflected celebration, I increasingly found instead a dispiriting story of fractured patterns and damaged health.

∿ But with the defeat of a cherished illusion can also come new possibilities for connection. So I discovered one August morning in the Green Mountains while climbing into a sugar-maple costume. A group of us were assembling in a parking lot beside the Robert Frost Trail in Ripton, getting ready for a five-day walk from Bread Loaf, where Frost summered in his latter years, to Burlington. This project was the brainchild of Bill McKibben, who is a Ripton resident in addition to being a leading writer and activist on climate change. Our goal was to raise awareness of climate change and its consequences.

Even in environmentally oriented Vermont, astonishingly little action had been taken to steer our economic and transportation systems away from dependence on fossil fuels. As Nicholas Kristoff wrote in a *The New York Times* op-ed piece, though global warming was the most important story of the century it never seemed to capture the headlines on a given day. Our little band hoped that, as we walked along Vermont's highways with our signs and held rallies in each town where we stopped for the night, our demonstrations would be vivid enough to engage our fellow citizens. At our concluding rally in Burlington we would ask Vermont politicians to sign on to the climate-change legislation that had been proposed by James Jeffords during his final session in the Senate.

In support of our attempt to get some press coverage, volunteers had come up the mountain on this first morning with a stack of signs for walkers and a couple of large cardboard boxes filled with costumes. I had just picked out a colorful sign saying "Sugarers to Save Maples" (though I would have preferred "Sugarmakers") when Sophie McKibben, the teenage daughter of Sue Halpern and Bill, shouted over that there was an outfit I needed to try on. I found that it was in three pieces. A long, dark-brown shift of cotton fell from my shoulders to the tops of my boots. Someone had put a lot of effort into indicating the characteristic fissures and texture of maple bark with a black Magic Marker. Toward the upper part of this garment, artificial maple leaves of yellow, orange, and red sprouted thickly, indicating the start of the tree's crown. A sturdy dowel was slid in across my shoulders to suggest branches within the mantle of leaves. And then there was the headpiece—much too grand a construction for the simple word "hat." Inside, it was a stiffened cone of fiberglass fabric. But that shape was totally obscured by a vivid explosion of leaves that rose almost a yard above the top of my head.

I donned this costume with a solemn sense of satisfaction in helping to bring some color to the march's first day. Despite the daunting realities of global climate change, we wanted to set a celebratory tone for our passage through the fields and villages that inspired us to action and gave us strength. Our hope was to incite solidarity, not to spread gloom. But as soon as I was suited up I realized this costume was not simply colorful. It was ludicrous, provoking laughter on all sides, from old friends and total strangers alike. Looking at the photographs of maple-me that subsequently appeared in various local newspapers and magazines, and that long continued to arrive in the mail from fellow marchers, I can see why my appearance in this tree suit struck so many as so ridiculous. One especially stupid-looking detail in these pictures is the broad, snow-white elastic band that anchors that weighty head-dress around my chin. It seems to shout, "Gawky home-made costume!" and to evoke an indulgent parent's efforts on behalf of a small child at Halloween. Even funnier, I have to admit, is the face peering from this towering swirl of leaves. My gray beard bristles around the prim white strap, while my eyes squint out through professorial little rimless glasses. I'm peering timidly into a crowd that finds me much, much funnier than I'd expected.

I didn't wear the maple get-up for very long after the opening speeches were over. The unyielding dowel and the head-dress's chafing interior would have been more than a little uncomfortable while descending Route 125 through the Middlebury River's dramatic gorge. But even for the hour or so I had it on, this costume transformed my outlook on both sugarmaking and conservation. Nothing stronger than Gatorade was being drunk in my vicinity, but between my costume and the half a dozen others scattered through the milling crowd, a sense of irrational exuberance took hold. Our symbolic celebration of the landscape lurched into the hilarity of an actual party.

I had just about gotten used to looking totally stupid when a radio reporter came up, laughing, and raised a microphone to my foliage. "Who are you?" Declaiming in my best Ent-like "Hoom-hoom," I found myself saying, "I am a sugar maple tree." His next question, after a pause, was rather more tentative. "And what are you doing *here*?" As I responded with "Global warming makes me v-e-r-y uncomfortable," I was expecting that our conversation would soon ratchet down into an out-of-role exchange about the march and its goals, but he was backing away nervously by now.

This antic encounter suddenly reminded me of how it had felt to wear a costume for Mardi Gras as a little boy in New Orleans. In particular, it brought to mind the Keystone Kops outfit, complete with hat and oversized buttons, that my grandmother had made for me when I was a shy six-year-old. Standing on the Canal Street parade route in this get-up, I was amazed to hear myself yelling for folks on the floats to pelt me with the beads, trinkets, and candy they were scattering to the crowd. My elaborate costume was (if I do say so) widely, if laughingly, admired. And I was totally happy to mug for strangers, as coached by my whispering grandmother— rocking back and forth on my heels and twirling my toy truncheon while holding my mom's hand on the other side. My blue uniform felt like the ticket to an expanded identity in this exciting, if also rather confusing, community festival.

Such strong childhood associations with New Orleans, here at the edge of the Green Mountain National Forest, quickly brought their second jolt of revelation. With winter shortening and the average onset of sugaring season in Vermont edging earlier into February, our own seasonal celebration in the woods was beginning to overlap with Mardi Gras. I saw for the first time that there was a parallel between this carnival, so important in Latin cultures around the world, and our tradition of sugaring in northern New England. The usual mundane routines get thrown out in favor of lively gatherings of friends and neighbors that bring shape to the circle of the year.

The lengthening days of February bring an air of expectancy

to the Vermont woods. This is the hinge between seasons, when northbound geese call overhead, jays flute their spring songs, chickadees whistle their shrill replies, and sugarmakers hold our breaths. We may have just a month or less to make a year's crop of maple syrup, but can't get started until the days begin to climb above freezing even as the temperatures continue to fall well below that mark at night. Only when these factors are both right will the sap begin to move. Precious weeks can pass before the necessary conditions are aligned. But there will come a morning when strong sunlight follows a frosty dawn and drops of sap begin to rattle into buckets through the spiles of tapped trees, or to bubble through translucent plastic tubing toward stainless-steel holding tanks. By nightfall there will be hundreds of gallons of sap needing to be boiled down—forty of sap for one of syrup—while they're still fresh and tasty. So much for the expectant hush. Now the sugarhouse explodes into noise and action, laughter and strategy, as family and friends pitch in and neighbors hike up the graveled path, lured by white clouds billowing through the louvered roof above the evaporator.

Members of our family take turns in a rocker by the firebox doors, underhanding a few long splits of wood into the furnace-roar every few minutes. We shield ourselves from the heat by wearing elbow-length electrician's gauntlets while laboring to keep the sap at a high boil. We can easily burn through seven or eight cords in a season, and some years we end up having to eke out our supply of fuel by cutting ash—whose wood can be used while still green. As the sugarhouse swirls with sweet, warm steam Rita and I prowl around the evaporator, waiting for the moment when we can begin to draw off syrup. Over and over, we climb up on wooden viewing platforms to make sure the levels in our pans are high enough to prevent scorching when the sugar content thickens. Toward the end of the day it can get pretty dark in this sugarhouse deep in the woods. So we often have to use a flashlight or headlamp when peering down into that galloping boil. Meanwhile, our son Matthew draws off sample after sample of near-syrup, scrupulously testing their viscosity with a floating hydrometer that bounces in a skinny metal cup.

When it's finally time to open up the spigot, we organize an assembly line at the linoleum counter beneath our western window. We filter and grade the syrup now, then reheat it to 180 degrees Fahrenheit in a small propane canner before filling, wiping down, and labeling a diverse collection of cans, jugs, and bottles. Often, the first several runs of the season are Fancy, followed by batches that darken to Grade A Medium Amber, Grade A Dark Amber, and Grade B, perhaps snapping back to a bit more Fancy at season's end. (The names of all these grades have been officially changed while I've been revising this book. Though the labels on our containers have accordingly been updated, however, I continue to perceive, and describe, the taste of syrup with reference to the traditional framework.) The fluctuating color and flavor express variations in the bacterial content of the sap as the spring comes on. Finally, as buds open and tree frogs start to sing, the sap takes on a musty taste that tells us we're through with making syrup for another year.

The festive hilarity of this season comes both from its long-awaited start and quick-step action, and from its close association with food and music. If there are still piles of snow beside the sugarhouse doors, people coming up the path will see the necks of beer bottles perk invitingly out at them. Inside, a team of volunteers may be making cups of strong sap-tea, eating a coffee cake sent up by a friend, or heating some chili on the Coleman stove stationed on a card table in the corner. At lulls in the action or when we have extra forces and people are spilling out into the dooryard, music will often surround the sugarhouse—especially when our fiddler son Caleb is on hand with some of his friends. Barred owls often add their notes as night comes on (*Hoo-hoo, hoo-hoo-aw!*) and coyotes occasionally join in from the ridge to our south.

Such celebrations represent not only an experience of release but also an opportunity to prepare for what comes next. Mardi Gras and sugaring can both help communities, as well as individuals, get through a dark time. They create a harmony that encompasses apparent opposites, offering a symbolically charged outburst of collective energy while clearing a space for composure and patience. Rita, with her Latin heritage and Catholic upbringing, has helped me glimpse this Vermont parallel with carnival-goers bolstering their resolve for the long austerity of Lent. Even in the midst of climate change, sugaring allows families like our own to hang in there during what might otherwise feel like the endless suspension of mud season. In each case, the focus is ultimately on renewal and spring.

Mardi Gras, as both a more broadly inclusive party than sugaring and a much wilder one, conveys an invitation to think of celebration as a cathartic preparation for personal and community transformation. Ash Wednesday, coming on the heels of Mardi Gras, ushers in Lent's forty days of repentance, atonement, and renewal. Citizens of the consumerist West confront the same basic challenge that has always been faced by the faithful during Lent: the need to restrain our appetites in the interest of reordering our spiritual priorities and individual practices alike. For both groups, a wild party might be just the thing to burn off indulgent energies—and perhaps to prepare for that special kind of mindfulness that can come with an aching head.

↬ Two paintings have strengthened this sense of a connection between the seasonal rhythm of loss and celebration and Rita's and my life in retirement. I stumbled on the first of these in the catalogue for an exhibition of the nineteenth-century American artist Eastman Johnson's sugaring paintings that had been mounted at the Clark Institute in Williamstown, Massachusetts. These monumental oils confirmed that sugaring, with its alchemy of sap into syrup, has *always* felt to New Englanders like a party—promising that, even when facing a long winter, life could still be sweet, like those puckery apples carefully stowed in their barrels of sawdust. They also showed, though, that when such local festivities have been pursued with an awareness of their connection to vaster political challenges and out of sympathy with other, far-flung communities, they can sometimes take on enhanced power and intensity.

Despite the fact that most of these paintings were produced in the 1860s, many details in Johnson's scenes were drawn particularly from his experience of sugaring while growing up near Fryeburg, Maine during the 1820s. Instead of an evaporator within a sugarhouse he thus depicts a huge black kettle suspended over a bonfire. Rather than being tapped into hanging buckets, the maples encircling that kettle dripped into wooden troughs set on the ground; the contents of those containers were then transferred into barrels on runners for transporting to the fire. Syrup would continue to thicken in the enormous cauldron shown by Johnson until it was ready to be ladled out into wooden forms, where it could then crystallize into cakes of sugar.

Johnson's paintings show logs being chopped and carried, containers of sap being transported to the fire, and a smoke-swirled clearing where most of the people seem to be drinking, dancing, and flirting, temporarily released from their usual chores. A work like "Party in Sugar Maple Camp" (c. 1861-1866) thus represents, as the catalogue to "Sugaring Off" says, a "bacchanal celebrating the end of winter." An especially striking connection with the festivities in our own Starksboro sugarbush comes in the figure of a fiddler sitting atop a pile of logs and playing for the carousers around the bonfire, just as our son Caleb's fiddling sometimes sings out over our own little clearing in the woods. I don't know what Johnson's fiddler was playing, but we hear tunes like "Soldier's Joy," "Haste to the Wedding," "Over the Waterfall," and a long skein of medleys and improvisations.

The experiences of delight and community can be amplified, as they were in New England's sugaring celebrations during the Civil War and again in the post-Katrina celebrations of Mardi Gras, by correspondingly strong feelings of protest and activism. In the wounded ecological conditions and confused social and economic status of sugaring today, celebration may in fact become more emotionally available within an *activist* context. In "A Party in the Maple Sugar Camp," as in many of Johnson's other paintings, the fiddler perched atop that towering pile of logs is African-American. This detail reinforces a crucial aspect of sugaring for the artist and his contemporaries. Abolitionists had long noted the link between cane sugar and slavery. As the exhibition's curator Brian Allen writes in the catalogue, "about two-thirds of the 20 million slaves taken from Africa to America labored to produce cane sugar, which was exported to Europe and later sold in urban American markets. Maple sugar had no such stigma." Allen continues, "Quakers and, later, a range of New Englanders deemed maple sugar 'innocent' precisely because it was not 'sprinkled with the tears and blood of slaves' but rather 'made by those who are happy and free.'"

The participants' delight in the "bacchanal" of sugaring was thus strengthened by its connection with strongly held political convictions. Making and consuming maple sugar helped rural families to remain mindful of the larger struggle of their time, and offered a way to express solidarity with the many young men from their own communities who were off fighting for the Union. Even though my earlier sense of sugaring's party in the woods came to feel simplistic in a time of global warming, I do still believe that such a combination of seasonal festivity and solidarity within a larger cause would be worthwhile to cultivate in sugaring today. Just as patriotism reinforced traditional New England practices during the

Civil War, the production of maple syrup can be aligned in our time with efforts to protect the forests, shorelines, agricultural plains, and cities of the whole world, and while doing so to seek a more equitable society. Such an ecological, and moral focus will only be possible to sustain, though, if we bear in mind the most encompassing problem of our own time—global climate change.

In my Vermont immigrant's ardor and my enthusiasm about sugaring I had conceived of our state's landscape as a sort of refugium, to use a biologist's term for isolated environments harboring "relict" species. From such refugia the surrounding landscape could be replenished, as it was after the retreat of glaciers from the denuded lower elevations of the New England landscape. But such a conception confined me within what the historian James Lindgren has called the realm of "idealized landscapes and wholesome images." The fact of the matter is that sugarmakers have long since been pulled into a landscape of complexity and confusion, a terrain of loss but also of promise for an enriched sense of community. While a place like Vermont can still feel like a green and pleasant realm to visitors and residents alike—one that is superficially remote from the congestion, stress, and sprawl afflicting so much of the country—we neverthless face a world in which every nation, state, and valley lies open to the same changing and disorienting sky. Rather than viewing this one living tradition as a hopeful example for the country as a whole, then, I now see sugaring as having been cast adrift in a melting land. Within this realm of loss, however, we may also discover a season of invigorating confluence.

An important vehicle of such confluence in my own life has been the liquid and melodious sound of the Irish flute, through which I have been led to meditate on the parallels between Vermont and Connemara while walking first in one of those landscapes then in the other. But one such similarity is in fact the historically ignorant and ecologically oblivious ways in which tourism has been promoted in both regions since the nineteenth-century. Seamus Deane has called attention, for instance, to Victorian celebrations of Ireland's sublime and picturesque scenery "from which the traces of a disastrous history [have] been removed or aggregated into the theme-parks . . ." Tim Robinson's writing represents above all a counter-impulse to such erasure. In testimony as harrowing as the story that Meliboeus offers to that holiday-maker Tityrus, Robinson insists on the pain inscribed in those ruined farmhouses and tumbled stone walls. Conversely, he asserts the irreplaceable value of the language, families, and communities shoved brusquely aside by the architects of empire. In her fine interview with Robinson, Christine Cusick refers to his relentless honesty about "fading and soon to be forgotten ways and words" as an "entropic shaming of the land."

From attentiveness to the real history of a place can arise an enhanced possibility for compassionate responses such as Tityrus makes to Meliboeus at the end of the first Eclogue. Instability and loss can get something started. Much of the diversity of Vermont's forests today comes from a "hypsithermal" warming interval 4,000 to 6,000 years ago, when southern species like hickories, chestnuts, and oaks forged north through the Connecticut River valley, becoming interspersed with northern hardwoods like maples, beech, and birch, as well as with our coniferous trees. It may be that the story we have to tell in Vermont today has less to do with the New England landscape's distinctiveness and separateness than it does with the possibilities for community in a new era of disorientation, exploration, dialogue, and diversity. Streams of local history and stories of traditional and sustainable practices converge with other streams in the welling expansiveness of a watershed. Maggie Brook, flowing through our family's sugarbush, joins with Baldwin Creek and the New Haven River, as they head north into Otter Creek, and then west through Dead Creek, into Lake Champlain. Continuing further through the Richelieu River and the St. Lawrence Seaway this company of waters eventually arrives at the sea.

Vermont's maple forests and sugaring practices, similarly, become ingredients in a new cultural mélange, along with stories and practices from as far away as Louisiana and Connemara. The struggle for environmental justice, so evident in New Orleans in the aftermath of Katrina and so stringently asserted in Tim Robinson's writing, needs to become more central to my own thinking about Vermont, conservation, and the Thoreauvian tradition of nature writing as well. Climate destabilization offers both a reason and a way to rethink the self-contained image of New England. And looking at all these matters through the lens of Mardi Gras brings a welcome access of zany energy, as I experienced when donning the tree suit.

Too often in discussions of environmental justice, there is a tone of judgmentalism and obligation. Conservationists and writers sometimes engage in this project with the solemnity of activists trying to do a hard thing. But when the indomitable hubbub of New Orleans echoes into the sugarbush, the sober conversation about sustainability and balance can morph into a wild party with great food and music. The sexy voltage of impromptu French-Quarter parades (all those revelers dressed as naughty nuns) suggests that a truly significant dialogue between nature and culture may be propelled more powerfully by humor, dancing, and desire than by a high-minded sense of obligation. Rather than struggling so hard with environmental ethics at an academic level, we might move more swiftly toward an ecologically informed society by celebrating the *erotics* of conservation. In Brian Friel's play *Translations*—to which I referred earlier in connection with Tim Robinson's attention to an effaced language of the land in Connemara—a touching and funny courtship between a British soldier and an Irish girl is carried out through an exchange of Irish place names. While this warm-hearted episode doesn't end well it does speak to the power of desire to help flesh out a world flattened by unfeeling power.

After Mardi Gras, the community "gets its ashes" and girds for the real work of discipline, self-restraint, and reverence. But the party that burns away indulgence may also be a portal into new possibilities for community. Both the festivities and their aftermath are motivated at the deepest level not by obligation but rather by desire. But too often the environmental conversation focuses on purity instead and seeks to approach that goal through externally enforced restrictions. At this time of disaster and confluence, we would do well to think of conservation as an invitation to a Creole celebration, a happy gathering of diverse constituencies in preparation for the real work.

The surprises of retirement, including the beginner's mind of Irish music and the lengthening shadows of illness, have been augmented for me by this latest encounter with the first Eclogue. Both music and illness are Rita's and my neighbors now, unanticipated presences at this table. They help me to understand that retirement is not only an opportunity to seek personal balance. It is also a preparation for expanded sympathy and hospitality, and for a more inclusive sense of community. As shadows fall from the highest mountains, our marriage is filled with more music than ever, buoying us with the same lilting rhythms that have long propelled dancers across a room. Whether in the wild melee of a party or in a living room with two musicians and a dog dozing on the rug between them, a few good tunes in company can help our shared and separate passages through life retain their bounce and sway. The tunes Rita and I share each evening are our musical equivalent of Mardi Gras. They sharpen our appetite for an approaching season of subtractions.

⮫ At the start of my graduate school experience we students of the humanities were required to take several language exams. Our Latin was tested with a couple of pages from the Anglo-Saxon chronicler known as the Venerable Bede. This was my introduction to Bede's famous passage comparing a human life to

... the swift flight of a sparrow through the house where you sit at supper in winter ... , while the fire blazes in the midst and the hall is warmed, but the wintry storms of rain or snow are raging abroad. The sparrow, flying in at one door and immediately out at another, whilst he is within, is safe from the wintry tempest, but after a short space of fair weather, he immediately vanishes out of our sight, passing from winter to winter again. So this life of man appears for a little while, but of what is to follow or what went before we know nothing at all. (Translation by A. M. Sellar, 1907)

Firelight and warmth are made more precious by the wintry dark, just as the dancing rhythms of sets in an Irish session are more vivid when interspersed with the unsettling spaciousness and rhythmic hesitations of slow airs like "The Month of January." As the concluding lines of that air remind its listeners, "For the green leaves they will wither and the branches all decay / and the beauty of a young man it soon will fade away." Long pause. Then it's back to tunes that lift our hearts and help to celebrate the moment, no matter what may be coming next.

⌁ I sent away for Fintan Vallely's splendid *Companion to Irish Traditional Music* out of a desire to know more about the history, the varieties, and the performers gathered at this musical feast. When the hefty volume arrived in the mail I found that its slipcover reproduced yet another nineteenth-century painting that spoke to my sense of a connection between sugaring season and Mardi Gras. "Snap Apple Night," by Daniel Maclise, depicts a harvest party at full throttle. A fiddler, a flute player, and a bodhran player are giving it their all on one side of the room, near a gray and apparently blind piper who just keeps playing while a convivial reveler tips ale into his mouth from a foaming tankard. "Snap Apple Night" was another term for Halloween, a moment in the year when the apple harvest was traditionally celebrated by bobbing for apples and also eating candy-apples. The canvas portrays party-goers of all ages as they flirt, kiss, bob, dandle babies, play cards, tell fortunes, eat, drink, and dance in a huge, firelit, and food-filled room.

Maclise was born in Cork, traveled to England in order to study painting, and was on a visit home when he attended this particular party in a large barn near Blarney in 1832. It's hard to look at this work without thinking of the Great Hunger and the flood of emigration that would come to Ireland within just a couple of decades. But even before the advent of those disasters hunger has always dogged the heels of harvest, and the question of how to eke out their stocks of food until the next year's growing season would have weighed heavily on Ireland's rural communities. For this one night, though, with a new supply of apples and cider fueling the party, the entire community could gather in a celebration amid firelight and shadow, a chiaroscuro like the blend of melancholy and effervescence in Irish music itself. This is the flickering wholeness to which Rita and I too have now come. While never offering a resolution, it nonetheless remains an opportunity for experiencing the balance between apparent oppositions in our lives. The only choice is to keep moving, buoyed up by the same lilting rhythm that pulls dancers and players forward measure by measure.

The surging rhythms of Irish dance music bring this musical analogy into high relief. In a couple of recent workshops Benedict and Hilari commented on what gives jigs their vitality. Just as weighting the *first* notes in each of a jig's triplets gives the tune its "swing," so too a "lift" can arise when the *third* notes of these little units are emphasized as well. Such lifting helps each measure flow right into the next one. I hear these pulsing accents as an unbroken Tah-da-Ya-Tah-da-Ya, with each Ya being as closely linked to the note that follows as it is to the two preceding ones. Such a cadence pulls revelers forward through Maclise's dancing shadows and amplifies their sense of a musical continuity between the seasons and the years. After a long winter's hush, first seedtime and then harvest will arrive. There will be food on the tables where community can be nourished, spaces cleared between them afterwards for a celebration.

Foregone Hillsides

ISLAND OF WOODS

I WAS WALKING UP A GRASSY SLOPE in the Burren on an
overcast September afternoon with the poet Moya Cannon.
To the other side of the road below us rose a facing hill. We
could hear the insistent voices of sheep across the valley, track
their southward drift whenever we turned round to stretch our
backs and vary our view from the close-cropped turf before us
and the scatter of wild garlic just coming into flower. As our
path continued a sparse flock of shrubs began to tuft up. Soon
after that we arrived at a zone where hazels grew amid a tumble
of boulders woolly with moss. There was a cave-mouth, too,
in this stony wrinkle of land situated south of Kinvara and
just below Eagles' Rock. Close to the cave, a spring welled up
through a crack in the limestone to fill a holy well festooned
with what seem to be Mardi Gras beads. A few laminated saints'
cards were displayed on nearby stones, while a tiny plastic troll
dangled by its pink hair from a branch.

Moya had led me to the cave because in the seventh-century Saint Colman MacDuagh had established his hermitage here. As we caught our breath she drew my attention to a number of hoof-shaped marks in the smooth stone at some distance from the cave mouth. They anchored an arresting tale of how once, on a chilly Easter morning, the saint and his acolyte knelt to pray for something to eat after the long austerities of Lent were finally over. Just as they did so, Colman's kinsman King Guaire was sitting down to a feast with his retinue at DunGuaire, near the present settlement of Kinvara. Suddenly, the laden plates lifted off the surface of their battered oak table and sailed over the treetops. Guaire's party saddled up and galloped after their disappearing dinner, forging up the same hillside we ourselves had just climbed and never taking their eyes off the flotilla of food advancing before them. They were sweating forward as the plates began to settle down in front of Colman and his companion. Then the whole company rattled to a halt. Their horses' hooves had stuck fast to the stone, preventing a nearer approach to the cave. Only when the saint and his young helper had finished their meal were the royal visitors allowed to continue toward them.

In Benedict and Hilari's workshop dedicated to the music of Clare we learned a fling called "Dunguaire" that brought a cheerful syncopation to this venerable saint's tale. There's a similarly light-hearted quality to the name by which the track between DunGuaire and the hermitage is known to this day: *Bothar na Mias*, the Road of the Dishes. And those intriguing imprints in the stone continue to be pondered by residents of the Burren and visitors alike as they stroll up that path for themselves on a pleasant afternoon. Different versions of the story work with this narrative topography in startlingly divergent ways, however. Early saints' tales were often vehicles for certifying the Irish Church's ascendancy after a period in which clerics and Druids contended for dominance. In one way of relating the cave to the hoof-marks, the king and his company set out to *recapture* their dinner but were so impressed by the saint's miracle-working power that they requested baptism by him then and there at the holy well. This account doubly dramatizes the emergent faith's superior power.

A different angle on the tale emerges in J. Fahey's 1893 *History of the Diocese of Kilmacduagh*. In that account, Guaire, already a believer, prayed before sitting down to his feast that it might go to support the work of some holy man. Then he and his company followed delightedly after the dishes to see who the beneficiary might be. But a question arises here about those miraculous marks where the horsemen slammed to a stop. Did Colman not recognize his pious cousin? Fahey's version, like the other one, stipulates that he waited to release Guaire's retinue until after his acolyte and he had finished their meal, and even then he did so only after an entreaty from the king.

As we reflected on the gaps and internal tensions that give this story the shadowy fascination of an ancient ballad, Moya Cannon mentioned that her naturalist friend Gordon D'Arcy could tell an altogether different story about the marks at which we were gazing. Similar puddled depressions may be found in parts of the Burren far from the saint's cave, he might point out. These are "solution hollows", marking where the fossils of brachiopods had surfaced and then been eroded away.

Leslie Marmon Silko, reflecting on the myths and chronicles adhering to boulders, buttes, arroyos, and other stony landmarks of northern New Mexico, has remarked how in an oral tradition one version of a given tale often corrects or fills out another way of telling it. It is inevitable that in a long-settled landscape like Ireland or the desert around her own people's home at Laguna Pueblo, a community's foundational tales will differ in dramatic ways depending on the identity and agenda of the teller. But as long as the story-telling remains a collective enterprise that focuses on enduring elements of the shared landscape, such varying accounts can combine to reinforce the people's sense of identity. As Silko writes, "The ancient Pueblo people sought a communal truth, not an absolute. For them this truth lived somewhere within the web of differing versions, disputes over minor points, outright contradictions tangling with old feuds and village rivalries." In the Burren, similarly, walking up in company to inspect those mysterious marks by Colman's cave unfolds the map for a widening conversation.

⤺ Two days after our outing to the cave, Moya and I were both heading to Galway to participate in a celebration of Tim Robinson's writing and maps. It turned out to be the first of several such programs, during the four years covered by this memoir, that marked the completion of his remarkable *Connemara* trilogy and also surveyed Robinson's projects leading up to that achievement. Professor Jane Conroy of the National University of Ireland at Galway was a lead organizer of the entire sequence of events. Though Rita was not able to join me on this occasion I still wanted to make the trip because of the ways Robinson had deepened my appreciation for the affinity between the whipsawed beauty of western Ireland and that of the Green Mountains.

Both regions experienced dramatic depopulation in the middle of the nineteenth-century, with emigration setting the seal, in one case, on famine and starvation; in the other, on heedless deforestation followed quickly by the American Civil War. In this part of Connacht and in Vermont alike, settlements and farms languished in the second half of the nineteenth century and the first half of the twentieth. In their quiet, old-fashioned character, though, both regions also came to symbolize a refreshing alternative to the rapid pace of modern life. This was the surprising upshot of large-scale abandonment. Robinson's writing insists, as noted earlier, that western Ireland should continue to be understood as a wounded landscape as well as a beautiful retreat. It is this perspective on the mysterious alignment of loss and recovery, suffering and compassion, that has most illuminated kindred realities in the ecological and cultural topography of my Vermont home.

Much of the program celebrating Robinson took place within the thick stone walls of the Druid Theatre in Galway's historical center. As writers, artists, and scholars rose one after another to talk about how his work had enriched their understanding of Ireland's land and culture, Tim and Máiréad sat decorously in the front row—holding their famously dry humor on a short leash and restraining their fidgets amid what must have sometimes seemed an interminable swell of praise. Finally, when it was his turn to stand up, he delivered a talk called "A Land Without Shortcuts." While his books on the Aran Islands and Connemara had asserted that loss and dislocation needed to be incorporated into any authentic affirmation of the landscape's meaning, Robinson was not focusing now on relics or memories. He was concerned, rather, about immediate dangers to fragile rural beauty from renewable-energy projects motivated by the dangers of global warming. I was especially struck by his talk, and challenged by it, because of its connection to controversies over wind power that are currently rending the environmental communities in both Ireland and Vermont.

I have long been, and continue to be, a passionate advocate of substituting renewable energy for fossil fuels. But Robinson's way of addressing the costs of such an approach helped me open my heart more fully to the concerns of Vermont neighbors with whom I disagreed about the installation of twenty-one wind turbines on a ridge in northern Vermont. His attention to loss in our rural regions' present and future as well as in our past also offered a more encompassing outlook on these wounded and recovering landscapes. Such a broad perspective suggested the possibility for respectful communication between what might have seemed sternly fortified counter-positions. Furthermore, coming so soon after the walk to Saint Colman's cave, his talk reverberated for me with the conflicting versions of Moya Cannon's story.

At the outset of his talk, Robinson described without reservation the crisis of climate change: "The globe is warming; we are facing into an era of floods, fires, famines; little doubt about it." Such direct acknowledgement of my own deepest fears helped me to be more receptive to his main point. Namely, that renewable energy installations in Connemara were bringing "a great leap forward in the mechanization of the countryside, unparalleled since the Industrial Revolution." With reference to new modes of energy production being proposed by Ireland's Green Party, he said that, "Leaving aside the unavoidable pollution caused by their manufacture, transport, installation and decommissioning, they are in operation grossly visually polluting. And where they go, no one else can go. They mean locked gates, culverted streams, barbed wire, foregone hillsides. These are the spoil-heaps of wind-mining." Referring to climate change and the development of renewable energy at the industrial scale as two "ditches" between which we were now skidding, he asked ". . . how much of the world do we have to destroy in order to save it?" Robinson's question was not rhetorical—a salvo launched in order to score points in a debate. Rather, it described a stark dilemma—neither indulging in polemic nor proposing a solution. Robinson's talk struck me as being essentially a lamentation for changes in a beloved landscape.

In Vermont, debate over recent wind projects has not always been marked by respectful recognition of opponents' perspectives. I have been angered as a supporter of wind-energy by the tendency of some opponents to describe politicians and environmental groups supporting such installations as corrupt, and as complicit in the corporate machinations of major players like Québec's Gaz Metro. But my own hot disagreement with such arguments drew on feelings of distress far broader than the current controversy. Namely, the many visible, and cumulative, changes in Vermont's climate and forests. It's equally true, though, that people who object to such installations feel wounded and betrayed by fellow environmentalists' apparent disregard of the ecological and scenic costs of erecting lines of massive wind turbines on largely undeveloped ridgelines. In addition, the alliance of our state agencies with a major Canadian utility company made them feel, as Meliboeus did, that their mountains of home had been expropriated by distant gods. This local story of polarization and regret was the context within which I listened to Tim Robinson's talk. It led me to speculate about whether, for a community as for an individual, shared grief might be able to offer a path beyond divisions.

One anecdote incorporated in Robinson's talk particularly struck me:

> A few years ago I flew out to the Aran Islands to participate in a debate on a proposed windfarm there. On the same flight was a vigorous young enthusiast from an alternative technologies firm. When we extricated ourselves from the cramped little flying pram of a plane and stretched ourselves in the island breeze, which carried a thousand miles of ocean and a million wildflowers to our nostrils, he sniffed it and said with delectation, 'Ah! Kilowatt-hours!'

That comical but at the same time chilling story recalled a passage from Book X of *Paradise Lost*. Adam and Eve have fallen and are about to be expelled from the Garden of Eden. Labor, suffering, and mortality are the lot bequeathed to their descendants—which is to say, us. Just at this juncture in the story, Sin and Death are following their father Satan into the newly fallen world, travelling on a highway that Death hammers out of the surrounding Chaos with his mace as they proceed. Like a vulture circling over the field where there is soon to be a battle, Milton writes, the "meager shadow" Death can already smell our unborn generations. We are for him just so many "living carcasses": ". . . with delight he snuffed the smell / Of mortal change on earth . . . / His nostril wide into the murky air, / Sagacious of his quarry from afar."

A scent in the air today foretells how the seasons and lands of vulnerable rural worlds may also soon be eaten up. Robinson's talk spoke both to those who are horrified by the impact of industrial scale wind turbines on delicate landscapes and fragile natural communities and to others transfixed by the evidence of Vermont's seasons, weather, and wildlife already being impaired by climate change, with the prospect of worse losses to come. Might we recently estranged Vermonters meet again at this keen edge of grief? The sorrow within Tim Robinson's talk in Galway helped defuse any impulse I might have had to charge furiously into the Vermont controversy over renewable energy. Instead, it prompted to me to ask whether we might find, if not unanimity, at least something approaching Silko's web of associated narratives. It rattled my controversial momentum, just as King Guaire's retainers came clanging to a halt before the hermit's cave. I returned to Vermont from this brief trip to the Burren and Galway prepared to walk forward quietly into our suffering landscape, in the company of neighbors whose passionate response to the new wind turbines might have seemed the opposite of my own.

⌒ So it came to pass, on a morning in May, that I was climbing up to the Lowell ridgeline with Tom Slayton, whose commentary about the wind-controversy there for Vermont Public Radio had recently caught my attention. In calling for a moratorium on further renewable-energy developments on ridgelines, Slayton made a proposal with which I strongly differed. But he also conveyed his love of that landscape in a way devoid of scorn or polemic. His central point was that our sense of place in Vermont is inseparable from our unspoiled mountains. Like Robinson, he knew enough to take climate change very seriously; like him, he also feared that attempts to mitigate it might in some cases cause grave damage to the landscape we were trying to save. I have known and admired Tom Slayton for many years, and we arranged to go together to see the changes to the Lowell Mountains through each other's eyes.

We set out after breakfast from his home in Montpelier and drove to the Nelson Farm in its lovely hanging valley above the town of Albany. The construction areas for the project, on a portion of the Lowell Ridge directly above the Nelsons' pastures and ponds, are off-limits to the general public now. But the family had flagged a trail up through their sugarbush that still took us to where we could see the graveled terraces being constructed for each of the massive turbines. These were of course much more massive than the foundation for any house or barn. One anti-Lowell Wind activist had described them as looking like ancient sacrificial sites, with the mountain itself as the victim.

Most visible for residents in nearby towns like Craftsbury are the white, slowly turning blades of the turbines. I myself find them beautiful, a feeling reinforced by an urgent desire to see our state make a more significant turning of its own toward renewable energy. What is by far the more noticeable impact up on the ridgeline, however, is the gravel being thickly applied at locations that have been bulldozed, and sometimes blasted, level. Two other serious effects can readily be inferred even when not directly observed. One is the severing of wildlife corridors by these emphatic breaks in the canopy and on the forest floor, while the other is a disruption of springs feeding into the Black River watershed. These are grievous losses for the natural fabric of our region. I must hold them in my mind, balancing my constant awareness that the sugar maples dominating those upper woods and anchoring its ecosystem will be among the first species eradicated if the next decade brings no substantial abatement of the carbon flowing into our planet's atmosphere. The lacy hemlocks gracing the ridges' rivulets will also certainly disappear.

Though the morning began bright and dry, rain was spattering down on us by the time we hiked back out of those woods in the early afternoon. Such shifting weather created a refreshing breeze that drew up the slope throughout our hike, giving us a respite from the mosquitoes and deer flies that can sometimes make exploring Vermont's woods during the late spring and early summer a frantic experience. After arriving at the ridgeline, we had timidly transgressed the heavily marked boundaries, stepping into a grey world across which trucks sped and heavy earth-movers rumbled. After gazing at this activity in silence for a few minutes, we turned our steps down-hill again toward the Nelsons' farm.

Because of the recent completion of one cycle of federal funding for such renewable energy projects, we may soon have an *economically* determined moratorium on more major installations for the foreseeable future. If that happens, lovers of the Vermont landscape must make of this an opportunity to move beyond our disagreements and assess the ecological and social costs (both here and elsewhere) of petroleum, coal, natural gas, hydro, and nuclear generation, as well as of emerging renewable technologies. Since all of them do have costs, and serious ones, we should also redouble our efforts at conservation and revisit our policies in the areas of housing, education, agriculture, and transportation with energy use in mind. In order to avoid a fatal skid into either of Tim Robinson's two ditches, this would be a good time to stop the speeding car and take a walk together as we deliberate about our alternatives. Inhabitants of North America, Europe and the Pacific Rim, especially, need to reconsider our profli-gate ways. Some of the most devastating impacts of climate change have come to impoverished populations, like those in Bangladesh and the mountains of Pakistan, who bear essen-tially no responsibility for global warming. Bill McKibben, after focusing on such injustices in his book *Eaarth,* con-cludes by urging that we learn "to live on the world we've cre-ated—lightly, carefully, gracefully."

〜 As we walked away from the sounds of heavy machinery we stopped from time to time to admire some of the early wild-flowers in the woods. The dominant color was white—the brilliant white petals of bunchberry, the delicate sprays of Canada Mayflower and foamflower. All along our path arose blackberry brambles too with their own profusion of white petals. I was reminded by them of the strong affinity between traditional music in western Ireland and in our part of New England, with "Blackberry Blossom" being one tune cherished in both places. I also thought about another white flower blooming at the edge of our Vermont woods in this season. Shadblow. I had been eying it all spring.

When shadblow blossoms in May, it marks Vermont's long-awaited turning from the long weeks of mud season toward the delicacy, color, and brevity of spring. A native of our region, shadblow (*Amelanchier canadensis*) most often appears around here as a leggy tree of twelve to twenty feet in height, growing in sparse woods or beside wet ground. Like those of apples and many other members of the rose family, its flowers have five white petals. But these are so slender and delicate that the crown of a tree in full blossom looks less like a cloud than like a drift of smoke—clinging together for just a moment before dissipating. To a hiker, or to a distracted driver who happens to glance from a car window at the right time, a flowering shadblow is all the more arresting because of its lovely recessiveness. Its emotional impact is less reminiscent of a trumpet-peal or a sudden shaft of light than of a mysterious, lingering scent.

The tree's name reflects its association with the annual migration of shad up the rivers of New England. Shad are anadromous, like salmon: they hatch in fresh water, but then spend most of their adult lives, and also reproduce, in the ocean. Just as the shadblow open, these namesake fish are beginning to return inland, after six or seven years in the salt, so that they can spawn in their native streams. This correlation between the flowering world and an ancient, dramatic migration prevails all the way from southeastern Canada down the mid-Atlantic coast. Over much of that range it also parallels the distinctive skein of bedrock shared by western Ireland, the Maritimes, and the northern Appalachians. Such a continuity among widely separated bioregions reflects the fact that, just as the blossoming is keyed to air temperature, so too the timing of anadromous fishes' migration relates closely to rising temperatures in the freshwater systems to which they are returning. As is true of so many ecological associations, this one between shad and shadblow mirrors a larger concord of climatic and chemical factors.

For both the indigenous Western Abenaki and the European settlers who put down roots in New England about four centuries years ago, the sudden arrival of these plentiful and delicious fish could not have come at a better time of year. Early spring has historically been a hungry season in the North, with the previous harvest largely exhausted, deer moving back up into the remote heights, and new crops just being planted. Reaching weights of four to ten pounds, shad are the largest members of the herring family, so that their value as a nutritional resource at this straitened moment in the calendar has been enormous. Both native communities and settlers could eat their fill, dry some fish for the future, and use still others to enrich the soil of fields beside the rivers. Attaching the fish's name to the tree thus expressed both hunger and hope in a flinty land where starvation was often a real danger.

Serviceberry is a second name used interchangeably with shadblow. Some scholars have traced it to the resemblance between this North American species and European members of the rose family that are called *Sorbus* in the Linnaean system and have been known as *sarviss* in the British Isles. Accordingly, serviceberry is often taken to be a corruption of its original New England name of sarvissberry. Be that as it may, New Englanders have also developed another deep connection between the name serviceberry and an aspect of local natural history as specific and significant as the timing of the shad run. Frosts extend deep into the soil here. When the white petals of shadblow appear, that has traditionally been taken to show that the ground has finally thawed enough for families to bury their winter's dead. The name serviceberry signals the possibility for long-deferred funeral services as eloquently as the name shadblow does the reappearance of shad in their native streams. Both speak to the ways in which recurrent natural phenomena have become both personally and culturally meaningful in this challenging landscape.

More recently, though, there is apprehensiveness connected with such seasonal modulations. Ecological disruptions, and in particular climate change, make of these two species gauges not just for the turning of the seasons and the continuation of our lives, but also for disruption in the living systems on which we depend. Starting in the late nineteenth century and continuing until fairly recently, the shad run was eliminated in most of northern New England. First came a wave of clear-cutting, including on the slopes of steep mountain valleys, that deposited enough silt in the streams to suppress many populations of fish. Then dams were built throughout southern New England for the purposes of powering mills, diverting water to cities for drinking, and controlling flooding. An unintended consequence of damming was the creation of barriers preventing anadromous species from making their ways back up many of their native streams. Emerging technologies were thus disrupting migrations that had been vital to human beings in this region for thousands of years.

An equally dramatic development in the last couple of decades, however, has been the reintroduction of shad to Vermont and our neighboring states. The water quality in our streams has been improved by policies that limit agricultural runoff as well as encourage hedge-rows and riparian fencing in order to impede erosion and limit cattle's ability to walk into fragile brooks. State environmental agencies have taken the lead in releasing fry into headwaters that traditionally supported shad, mandating removal of some dams altogether, and installing more effective fish ladders in those that are allowed to remain. Though the numbers of returning fish are still in the tens of thousands rather than the millions found at the time of European settlement, there is reason to hope that they may recover more substantially when the fish hatched a few years ago in restocked streams begin to make their way back to them from the sea.

The return of shad to Vermont—like the return of peregrine falcons to our family's own town of Bristol, thanks to Rachel Carson's leadership in restricting agricultural applications of DDT—inspires feelings of chastened hope. An awareness of ecological fragility in the face of human carelessness is coupled with experiences of reversing such damage through scientifically informed efforts of restoration. The return of iconic species like shad and peregrines reinforces our potential for a deeper sense of emotional, ethical, and social affiliation with our home landscapes.

The particular associations of the name serviceberry, however, continue to make it too a challenging seasonal marker now that climate change has had such a severe impact at our northerly latitude. Disastrous floods struck valleys to the east of the Green Mountains in the wake of 2011's Tropical Storm Irene, while the transition from winter to spring was so unseasonal and intermittent in 2012 as to truncate the sugaring season. Temperatures climbed into the eighties in early March and trees began to leaf weeks earlier than usual. This meant that when the temperatures dropped again at the end of that month, the sap was no longer sweet enough to boil down into delectable syrup. Many family-scale producers, like our own Maggie Brook operation, made barely a third of the usual crop. When the shadblow blossomed and frozen country roads became muddy and rutted, we had long since pulled our taps. What had historically been a marker of predictable transition, in other words, now felt like a token of loss, another disorienting and discouraging manifestation, like the dimming of our colors when the fall foliage came, of living in an unmoored world.

↶ The tune in my ears now, as I draw together in memory these hikes with friends in the Burren and the Northeast Kingdom, is Liz Carroll's "Island of Woods." The long history and ancient tonalities of Irish music, as represented by a tune like "Langstrom Pony," continue to renew themselves through compositions by contemporary musicians steeped in the traditional idiom. Josie McDermott served as an intermediary for Catherine McEvoy, and her students around the world, between the musical heritage her immigrant parents had borne with them and the Birmingham in which she grew up. Carroll, the daughter herself of Irish immigrants, has contributed powerful new tunes to this tradition from her home in Chicago. Among her many celebrated compositions, one of the most beloved is "Island of Woods."

It's a tune Rita and I heard for the first time at one of the small, informal sessions in Jonathan Leonard's airy living room. Though we share a sufficient core of tunes, it quite often happens that just a couple of musicians out of a group of eight or nine will play a set that only they know. It makes for a pleasant rhythm to lean forward to perform, then sit back to enjoy someone else's favorite tunes. "Island of Woods" was introduced in this context by Maria Wicker and Carolyn Buckley, two talented flute players in the circle. Their sweet tone, fluid rolls, and artfully sustained notes magnified the sad beauty of a tune that begins with a descent through the notes D, C#, B, with the B prolonged before going down over and over to an A that is played four times before finally settling on low D to end the phrase. It feels as if the melody has sunk under weighty emotional gravity from which it can't easily escape. Then almost the identical heartbreaking strain is played again, but this time going *up* repeatedly from the A to a B. To my ear, the contrast between those first repeated notes and the second sequence that shifts the repetitions up a single tone establishes the character of the whole piece. Like the substitution of C-natural for C# in "Langstrom Pony," this deliberate and highly noticeable choice reinforces the presence of a countercurrent near the end of the tune. In the second half of the tune's A-part the melody slides up to a high G before descending forcefully, by way of repeated D-C#-A triplets, to the lower E that grounds the tune.

LINK: *Island of Woods*

Here's what it sounds like.

"Island of Woods" was so simple and compelling that it went straight to our hearts. Maria and Carolyn told us that if we wanted to learn it we could just check out one of the many versions on YouTube featuring performances by Liz Carroll herself. She was often accompanied in such videos by guitar players, including the remarkable John Doyle. One of the aspects of her playing that made these renditions so powerful was her remarkable emphasis on the repetitions we had already noticed at the session. Rather than simply moving deliberately through the reiterated notes, she leaned into them dramatically—seeming almost to give way to those first heavy A's and B's before forging on. In connection with one of these performances, Carroll remarks that "Island of Woods" is an ancient name for Ireland, though she goes on to add that today a different name like "Land of Green Pastures" might be more fitting. In Ireland, as in Scotland, almost all the forests were destroyed long ago. Both the ship-building Vikings who settled on that island so early and the British Navy were avid for the famous Irish oaks, while centuries of grazing sheep guaranteed that the razed woods would not be returning.

As I've commented more than once, it's important to press lightly on the names of Irish tunes, many of which seem either whimsical or downright baffling. But in this case, especially given Liz Carroll's own comments, it's hard to avoid feeling the relevance of her title to the endangered forests of Vermont. They have recovered strongly both from the clear-cutting that made Vermont an ecological wasteland in the early nineteenth century and from the sheep industry that briefly flourished thereafter. But today climate change ensures that the forests as we have known them will not survive.

Hiking in the Lowell Range with Tom Slayton I kept hearing the echoes of those first three descending notes in "Island of Woods." Were they a lamentation, a eulogy? What tunes might they flow into next in this landscape of loss so much vaster than the span of human mortality? Though the rhythm of "Island of Woods" seems almost to falter in those opening phrases, it then recovers the stately tempo of a slow reel and the triplets with which it finishes feel defiant. What the music tells us is that those vanished forests may at least still flourish in our hearts, *and in this tune.*

Music is required if we are to move forward resolutely, in

the face of challenges that first make us falter, and in order to foster community when disagreements push neighbors apart. How else has Ireland endured such a history? We require, today, an activism that sings of what it loves. When hiking through Vermont's woods in late fall I have often recalled Frost's "Reluctance," which ends with this stanza:

Ah, when to the heart of man
Was it ever less than a treason
To go with the drift of things,
To yield with a grace to reason,
And bow and accept the end
Of a love or a season?

I understand that impulse to resist even unavoidable change, lest too ready an acceptance seem a betrayal. But, as the poet himself comes to affirm over the half-century of his writing that follows this poem, our only choice is finally to move forward into the next season while doing our best to serve and celebrate what we hold most dear.

↪ Disruption of ecological sequences that were once attuned to what Linnaeus called "the floral calendar" is one of the griefs of climate instability. But beloved flowers do continue to return, offering gauges not only for what we have lost but also for what endures, and what may be restored. Such recovery will neither be quick nor complete but it may nonetheless orient us to a more sustainable vision of community with what David

Abram has called the more-than-human world. Even when spring slips out of kilter, the flowering world can help us to affirm the bonds of love when we might otherwise have fallen mute. In "Flowers at Loughcrew," from her collection *Hands,* Moya Cannon reflects on the fossil pollen found at prehistoric burial sites, with its evidence that flowers have immemorially solemnized and adorned our relinquishment of the dead. Such discoveries show that the blossoming world has long lifted up our narrative of loss, making of it "our ceremony of grief / attended by what is most beautiful, / most fragrant on this earth."

This shuttle of dread and hope reminds me of Tim Robinson's resonant description of Connemara's "foregone hillsides." "Foregone" is one of those words that looks both backward and forward. Such hillsides are already in the past for Robinson, their delicate beauty extinguished by massive industrialization. But "foregone" can also refer to the future, the dictionary tells us—as in the phrase "a foregone conclusion." Severe and challenging climate change is at this point inevitable. It is equally certain, given the much greater diffuseness of non-fossil resources, that efforts to harvest renewable sources of energy will be at a scale alarming to many lovers of rural regions. There will be no easy solution to our present crisis.

Grief does not guarantee that people will arrive at a creative response to loss, but it does hold open such a possibility. For this reason, I incline toward the perhaps less canonical reading of Saint Colman and the Road of the Dishes, in which hostile warriors are halted in their tracks and then baptized. When the horses of anger are jerked to a stop under bewildering circumstances, there can be an opportunity for "conversion," turning together from our adamant agendas toward awareness of the turning earth. For those famished riders making their way up to the saint's cave, the swerve from intention created an unexpected space for deeper encounter. As serviceberry has long shown, spring can be a time for renewal as well as grief, with both emotions enacted in the single action of burying the winter's dead. Such a unitary accomplishment may well be harder to achieve now, as we search out new connections between our human projects and the disrupted but still flowering world. In both Ireland and Vermont, we will have to falter together toward a collective narrative grounded in memory and the land. Only by reconciling conflicting stories of our place and relinquishing the satisfactions of blame and righteousness will we be able to sustain ourselves as communities in a shadowed time.

Windings

THE PEACOCK'S FEATHER

ONCE, WHEN A CLASS OF Bread Loaf School of English students and I were ambling southward on Vermont's Long Trail, we encountered a manic through-hiker. Mud-spattered and rumpled from a week on the trail, we were carrying huge, clumsy backpacks and stopping frequently to write or draw in our journals. He came running up the trail with a svelte pack that hugged his spine like a soft Aqua-Lung and a clear tube leading from it to his mouth so that he wouldn't have to grapple with a clunky water bottle. His greeting, even before coming to a complete stop, was "How much do your boots weigh? Mine weigh fourteen ounces." Then, after telling us he hoped to finish the whole trail in a week rather than the usual seventeen days, he sprang off through the trees like Daniel Day-Lewis (minus the flintlock) at the beginning of *The Last of the Mohicans*. Beyond being on the clock, he must have realized there wasn't much potential for a good seminar on high-tech equipment in our gaggle of seedy, slow-moving teachers.

Though it was amusing to see someone speeding through those beautiful mountains with eyes only for his own boots, I must admit to feeling the allure of spiffy equipment in my own heart. It goes with being an enthusiastic hobbyist. The tools of our ardent avocations are like saints' icons. They are emblems that tell the world and ourselves who we are, and also how far we've made it up the trail of aspiration. Even if special implements are not necessary we invent them. When I started running cross-country in high school everyone just wore flat, white tennis shoes. Then a wide variety of waffle-soled, ergonomic, and anti-pronation (as well as much more expensive) shoes began to appear on the shelves. I was susceptible to their charms, and poring over the annual issue of *Runner's World* that reviewed each new cohort of shoes definitely influenced my decisions about what brand to buy next. Once, when I stopped by a sportshoe outlet to get some new socks, I grabbed a pair of cross-training socks with specially reinforced toes and heels and carried them to the register. In ringing them up the young salesman said admiringly, "Those are some serious socks!" For weeks after that a glow of self-satisfaction (enhanced by the virtuous smell of exercise that also wafted out) returned to me whenever I unzipped my gym bag and kitted up for a run.

Musicians are second to none when it comes to obsessing over their icons—which is to say, their instruments. More than once I've walked into a new session only to have another flute player literally run over like that trail-crazy and ask, "Who made your flute?" The ultimate equipment fetishists of all may be the concertina players and, according to Rita, the male concertinists in particular. One workshop she attended was dominated by men who were engineers or worked in computer-related fields. Though perfectly pleasant in most of their interactions, they took endless delight in describing the specific materials, weights, tolerances, and resistances of their instruments. And whatever makes they may have played themselves, they had a vast amount of information, and decided opinions, about all the other new or vintage instruments owned by members of the group. Such obsessiveness may well be encouraged by two unique characteristics of the concertina. For one thing, what with the various levers, springs, and pads arrayed below each button and the many little gores of leather and cardboard reinforcing the corners of its intricate bellows, a concertina can have over a thousand parts. Additional incentives to fretful fascination with the instrument include the facts that you can't really watch your fingers, that the notes on a given side are not arranged from high to low as on a piano keyboard, and that the note sounded by a particular button is different on the press and on the draw. The technical aspect of playing the concertina thus remains a preoccupation for far longer than with, say, the flute.

A couple of years ago I did in fact order a second, keyed flute from Yolanta and Forbes Christie, in the hope of getting a more solid low F, a clearer C-natural than I produce by cross-fingering, and a high G# truer than I can usually manage by half-holing. Until that point my only experience as a player had been with the radical simplicity of a conical wooden flute and its three unadorned sections. The top one of these includes a tuning slide and an embouchure hole, six fingered holes are drilled into the middle piece, while two vestigial, unplayed holes have been retained for resonance on the foot joint. The middle section also has a tenon on either end—an extension of reduced diameter that slips into the corresponding sockets of the head and foot joints. But even with this relatively plain wooden tube there was one important design option to ponder when I was earlier choosing which kind of unkeyed flute to purchase. Some premium flutes have a thin layer of cork wrapped around the tenon while other instruments of similar quality have thread wound closely around it instead. The cork is lubricated by the same kind of cork-grease also used in the joints of a clarinet, the thread by a variety of proprietary beeswax compounds. There are passionate opinions in the flute-playing community about the relative virtues of cork and windings, and the most outstanding artisans may well choose to use either system on the instruments they construct.

I've become a partisan of thread myself, even though it can present a bit of trouble to adjust it in both winter and summer. As the woodstove fires up with the coming of colder days and nights, the humidity level within a house drops and a flute's wood shrinks. When temperatures finally rise again, so that the windows can be flung open and the moist air can swirl back inside, a flute's diameter expands. Such seasonal fluctuations require that the thread be rewound more loosely in winter, for more bulk, while in summer a tighter, more compact winding is appropriate. One compensation for these continual little adjustments, however, is that one's flute can always have a perfectly snug fit. Besides, there's a certain modest element of craftsmanship involved in the process of unwinding and rewinding that can make a player feel like a participant in the foreordained and perpetual honing of a marvelously refined instrument. My own inclination to go for the windings was established in the first summer Rita and I attended the Catskills Irish Arts Week. Every morning I would drive from our room at Gavin's, the old-fashioned inn where we were staying, to park beside the rambling wooden structure where the Arts Week had its headquarters. I had just reached the point of wanting to trade in my original mail-order flute, so I fell into the habit, before crossing the street to the pub where our flute workshop would be meeting, of visiting the headquarters' wrap-around porch where Forbes and Yolanta were displaying their flutes.

Forbes has a bright eye and a ready smile, but is (at least on first acquaintance) a man of few words, while Yola is more talkative and sociable. She was thus the one I most often conversed with when stopping by to try out their various instruments on what became part of my daily routine. Increasingly I was drawn to a blackwood Pratten model with an ornamental disk of African olivewood inserted at the top of the head joint. The finish was deep and glossy, the lines clean. What's more, even when a neophyte like me played it, the lower register was dark and vibrant. Reader, I bought it. Part of the pleasure of doing so was that, over the week, the Christies and we also became friends. Last year they drove down to Bristol to have American Thanksgiving with us, while the year before we visited them for Canadian Thanksgiving at their home in Shelburne, Nova Scotia en route to the Celtic Colours festival in Cape Breton.

Throughout those first encounters in the Catskills, when I was playing their glorious Windward flutes and conversing with Yola about music, our families, and a wild scatter of other topics, she was deftly installing and adjusting the windings on various flutes still in process that they had brought along. The thread the Christies use is waxed silk, and Yola winds it onto each new instrument's tenons from a slender olivewood bobbin that Forbes turned on his lathe for this purpose. Holding one end of the bobbin between the thumb and forefinger of her right hand she begins by anchoring the thread's loose end to the recessed segment of the tenon with a bead of their own thick beeswax compound, then winding it into the recessed space with machine-like regularity. Before the winding has begun one can observe a series of little grooves, called combings, that have been incised in the tenon to stabilize the first layer of silk. These turn out upon closer inspection to be a continuous spiral rather than individual rings. The combings offer Yolanta "a good tooth" as she starts off by anchoring the windings with a thicker gauge of thread. Upon completing that stage of the process she consolidates this foundation by gently melting the beeswax in which it is embedded. Then she switches to a thinner diameter of silk.

The recessed portion of the tenon is soon filled with a shiny band of winding that rises just above the adjacent wooden surface. After arriving at this point Yolanta works wax liberally into the winding as a whole. The delicious aroma of this final application, which comes from Windward's distinctive mixture of beeswax and mint, rises faintly to my nose each time I twist the sections of my flute together or apart, always turning the piece in my right hand clockwise so that the threads are pulled together rather than separated. When I've bumped into Yola again in the years since buying my flute she is always happy to check out the windings and tutor me again on making seasonal adjustments. As she briskly winds and unwinds each delicate skein of thread, while always maintaining a friendly patter, she sometimes seems a cheerful younger sibling of those three Sisters who stretch and cut our mortal threads.

↵ The mesmerizing pattern in which shiny filaments of silk are wound and then unwound from the tenons of a flute has become linked for me with the words *helix* and *gene*. This terminology relates not only to the spiral form of the virus that was likely behind my polymyalgia during the first two years of retirement. More pressingly, it pertains to the mutation of Rita's DNA that has caused her ataxia. When I began teaching at Middlebury College in 1973 I intended—as soon as I had found my footing in the pedagogical equivalent of those combings in the tenons—to audit one science course every semester. This would have complemented my background in literature and languages. It never happened, though, since the semesters seemed just to get busier and busier. So now, when concerned and confused about these unforeseen challenges to our health, I am forced to consult my new best friend Google about both the specific maladies and their broader genetic context. In the course of one recent search Google's room-mate Wikipedia defined "helix" for me as

> a type of smooth space curve, *i. e.*, a curve in three-dimensional space. It has the property that the tangent line at any point makes a constant angle with a fixed line called the axis. Examples of helixes [sic] are coil springs and the handrails of spiral staircases . . . Helices are important in biology, as the DNA molecule is formed as two intertwined helices, and many proteins have helical substructures, known as alpha helices.

I was also informed that this word derives from the Greek for "twisted" or "curved," as well as that a helix is either right-handed or left-handed, even if one's perspective on it is flipped. The helical windings that Yolanta casts so evenly and snugly onto the flute are left-handed. That means if you look down the barrel of the instrument while revolving it clockwise the helix will spin toward you.

I had actually begun reflecting about the genetics of Irish music back when hearing Chris Norman describe "Langstrom Pony" as a "super-tune," one that was carried into many other tunes and national traditions by the permutations and com-binations of its rudimentary forms. This concept made me think in turn of Richard Dawkins's neo-Darwinist assertion in *The Selfish Gene* that genes, not species, are the real com-petitors for biological dominance. In the introduction to that volume Dawkins approvingly quotes J. S. B. Haldane's remark that no answer to the question "What is man?" from before 1859 (when *The Origin of Species* was published) deserves our attention. So much for the Book of Job, *Hamlet*, and *Faust*! Dawkins relents toward the end of his book, though, and coins the term *meme* to describe a cultural unit of information comparable to the packets of biological information in genes. Cooking pots with handles and the tripartite sonata form in classical symphonies are examples of memes perpetuating themselves down through the centuries. Dance forms like jigs, reels, and hornpipes are musical memes too. Instruments like concertinas and thread-wound flutes similarly fit the definition, as they manage to replicate themselves in one human generation after another.

I once attended a workshop at Camp Common Ground in Starksboro called the Northeast Heritage Music Camp. Participants explored the Irish, Québécois, and Appalachian heritages that have all strongly influenced traditional music in our region. The category of traditional, as opposed to classical, music covers a wide range of tunes and styles that are passed down the generations not in published form, but instead through a person-to-person transmission of listening, imitating, and memorizing. The inevitable mutations within such replication are often referred to as "the folk process"— by which musicians within a the larger landscape of Irish or Appalachian music, for example, develop regional or individual styles through both their fondness for certain innovative tonalities or rhythms and their composition of new tunes. In acknowledging the players from whom they learned particular tunes, Irish musicians also implicitly identify themselves with one or another of the closely associated yet still clearly distinguished traditions of East Clare or West Clare, East Galway or

West Galway, Roscommon or Sligo. Such fine delineations are like the intricate branchings of an evolutionary tree from its common trunk.

Useful mutations (like more or less skin pigmentation for human populations living in hotter or colder climates) are introduced by various factors, one of which is viruses. Though they have no cells of their own, viruses play an essential role in transferring genetic material from one cellular organism to another. The polymyalgia that hobbled my original retirement plans was also in all likelihood viral, according to my rheumatologist Dr. Dier. It belonged to the class of autoimmune disorders, so that the stiffness and pain in my shoulders and hips came from the antibodies crowding in to counteract an invading virus. While I was waiting for that invader to gallop away, like Napoleon abandoning looted and burnt-out Moscow, my inflammation was reduced by mainlining Prednisone and Ibuprofen. I look back on this two-year process of illness and recovery now as just another left-handed helical strain, like the adenovirus, winding its way into my body like tenons socketing stiffly into the headjoint and footjoint of my flute, then gradually loosening its hold under the unwinding, influence of Prednisone.

Such connections are much more in my mind now, since Rita's diagnosis with a condition that can be mapped quite specifically on the double helix of a patient's DNA. While checking out a website called *Genetics Home Reference* late one night I found that the cause of this particular ataxia is a mutation in the CACNA1A gene, which normally helps to form channels in which calcium atoms may be transported across cell membranes, as required for signaling between the brain and other parts of the nervous system.

> The CACNA1A gene mutations that cause SCA6 involve a DNA segment known as a CAG trinucleotide repeat. This segment is made up of a series of three DNA building blocks (cytosine, adenine, and guanine) that appear multiple times in a row. Normally, the CAG segment is repeated 4 to 18 times within the gene. People with 20 repeats tend to experience signs and symptoms of SCA6 beginning in late adulthood, while people with a larger number of repeats have signs and symptoms from mid-adulthood.

One's SCA6 "number" refers to this factor of CAG repeats. For Rita the number is 22. Diagrams in the various online resources and publications I have seen show the over-repetition of the CAG segment as a darkened portion of these helical, chromosomal windings within one's cells.

The third element for me in this trinucleotide structure of dread is Alzheimer's, from which my father died and which itself has a genetic correlation. His own form of the disease, late-onset Alzheimer's, is often associated with an allele, or genetic expression, called APOE e4. This is a mutation of the alipoprotein E gene, which normally helps carry cholesterol and other kinds of fat in the bloodstream. The e4 mutation is called a "risk-factor" gene, since it doesn't necessarily mean that one who carries it will develop Alzheimer's. Still, I got a sinking feeling about my outlook when, several years ago, I was discussing the disease with our friend Sue Halpern, who'd just published a book about it. She mentioned that, with my runner's build, I wasn't a likely candidate for Alzheimer's. But when I told her that my father had died of it she simply said, "Oh."

↜ My father was a serene and kindly person, whose equanimity exemplified for me the *I Ching's* "superior man." From his impoverished boyhood and emotionally abusive mother in southern Mississippi through his experiences of wading through gore as a member of the 82nd Airborne at Omaha Beach, Operation Market Garden, and the Battle of the Bulge, he flowed like water through the gaps and deep places. His good cheer reflected both his expansive historical perspective and the inner resources that made reading, music, and conversation so deeply satisfying for him. His benign unflappability was always a given for me while growing up. When I was six and we were far out in the Gulf of Mexico in a borrowed rowboat, the water suddenly welled through those dry old planks and the hull filled and sank. Dad calmly said to get on his back, after which he swam the two of us back to the dock. The shore was so distant when the swim started that we couldn't even make out our little rented cabin at first. Yet I can still remember my feeling of total security, clinging to the strong muscles of his shoulders as we glided home together over the deep.

Even as Alzheimer's began to affect him in his early seventies, stripping away words from his wonderful vocabulary by the handfuls, he would simply pause, as if puzzling briefly over the morning crossword puzzle, then bring forth a synonym for the word he couldn't come up with. Once, when he ran into trouble with a sentence that had clearly been headed toward "life preserver," he reached back smilingly into his word-trove and picked out "personal flotation device." He took this obstacle as another occasion on which to amuse and encourage his companions with a playful spirit. Little by little, though, the chasms between his words grew too wide for such improvised bridges to traverse and his speaking dwindled away almost entirely.

As it turned out, though, even at this stage he could sing beautifully. Members of the Tiburon Baptist Church would stop by the nursing home and sing hymns with him in his room. Song after song, he remembered all the words, and even the harmonies. But when he turned seventy-six and our family assembled at the nursing home for a party, our attempt to sing "Happy Birthday" to him disclosed that we had crossed yet another line. We wheeled him into the social hall that we had decorated with balloons and where we had set out cake and dishes on the table, and when we began to sing, his face crumpled with fear and confusion. Those were emotions I never could have associated with him under any circumstances, but there they were. We quickly took Dad back into his own quiet room, and from then on restricted our visits to simple, one-on-one interactions.

He did still try to speak on a few occasions. Once, when I had flown out from Vermont for the week that turned out to be our final visit, I was sitting by his bedside holding his hand when he opened his eyes, looked up at me and began, "John is." Very slowly, he began to spell. "B. E. L. O. " Long pause, then "O. F." When I asked, "beloof"? He smiled a tired, sweet smile.

I thought, or wanted to think, that the word he'd been headed toward was "beloved," and that he wanted to say he loved me. I said, "I love you too, Dad." The very last thing he ever said in my hearing, at the end of that same week, was the declaration, "Things change." I was startled by this complete sentence, and blurted out, "And why not?" At which point he repeated my own words laughingly, "And why not? And why not?"

In Jerome Groopman's "Medical Dispatch" about Alzheimer's in a *New Yorker* article entitled "Before Night Falls," he quotes Martin Samuels, head of neurology at Brigham and Women's Hospital, as asking, "If we lived long enough, would we all become demented, with plaques and tangles? Is Alzheimer's just another name for aging?" Even beyond the possibility of becoming afflicted by particular medical challenges like Alzheimer's, there can be a more generalized dread in the aging process. As toenails thicken, ears ring, and elbows sag, one notices a genetic unwinding, a gradual disassembly that will eventually leave us entirely undone. But these same changes, rather than taking the form of morbid self-consciousness, can also be openings to a larger dimension of awareness. Just as the last sentences my father spoke remain among the most memorable things he ever said to me, so too this time with Rita since her ataxia was diagnosed feels like one of the most precious moments in our marriage. Playing the concertina and flute together has been not only refreshing but also restorative.

There's always been a quality of goofy hopefulness in this commitment we've made to Irish music in retirement. It not only balances but in a significant measure also supplants that creeping sense of dread. Not permanently, it's true. Yet even so, again and again. Disassembling and reassembling my flute a couple of times a day—with the sweet odor of beeswax hanging in the air like the fragrance of new-mown hay drifting down North Street on a June evening—I experience a momentary sense of renewal. Winding, unwinding, and rewinding the tenons of my flute similarly gives me a sense that adjustments are always possible. The fact that things change need not leave one downcast.

⇀ I stipulated at the beginning of this book that, despite all the silken threads that bind Irish music and our marriage together now, this book would be about picking up the flute, not the concertina. That's the only instrument and experience I really know about firsthand. That said, an especially hopeful experience of adjustment and restoration in our new musical life was the terrifying, but ultimately successful, repair of Rita's concertina. While I was awaiting delivery of my keyed Windward flute, she was eagerly anticipating her own custom-made concertina from the Kentucky maker Wally Carroll. Since its arrival I've been fascinated by this jewel of an instrument, with its figured amboynia on the scrollwork ends, its cunningly recessed bellows, its brass buttons, and a slightly narrower span than normal that makes it delightful for Rita to cradle between her hands while playing. The tone produced by its double-beveled steel reeds, too, is vibrant and satisfying for player and listener alike. So when, within a year after Rita received it, first one, then two of the notes began to sound strangled, she felt mortified and downcast by the revelation that, here too, nothing gold could stay. Finally, though, we nerved ourselves up to try fixing it together, with the help of a photocopied sheet about repairing concertinas she had once picked up at a workshop.

First she unscrewed the six inset brass screws around one of the hexagonal end pieces, with me steadying the instrument since the strap and buttons didn't leave the other end a level place on which to rest it. She wielded a small, flat-bladed screwdriver with the greatest of care in order to avoid any scratches in the wood, then breathlessly lifted off the scrollwork peg cover. Then, fitting her fingertip into a hole in the thin wooden plate to which the instrument's complex metal apparatus was attached, she drew that out too. It was terrifying to assume responsibility for such intricacy. We were both somewhat comforted, though, by the fact that each reedboard had a letter L or R at one corner showing what side of the instrument it belonged on and in what orientation it needed to be refitted. Finely engraved on each reed, too, was the note it produced. The notes we hoped to repair, a C and a G#, were on opposite sides of the instrument, and thus required us to remove each end in turn.

An inch-wide strip of thin, hard-finish paper came with the concertina for just this purpose. Off sounds may be caused by a slight looseness between the narrow, tapering lozenges of brass onto which each reed is set and the slots radiating around the wooden reedboard's margin into which they in turn are fitted. One needs to slide the individual reed out a bit on its shoe, then snip off a tiny piece of that special paper and hold it in place with tweezers while sliding the reed snugly back over it. We carried out this fine maneuver with trembling intensity, even I whose only job was to hold the concertina while Rita operated, and when it was totally reassembled both notes were back to their expected perfection. Unfortunately, a different note, a high G, began to misbehave at this point. But we took a couple of calming breaths, opened the patient back up, and carried out the same procedure on yet a third reed. Not only has the concertina sounded wonderful ever since, but we now know that even if similar problems should develop in the future there is a way to fix them.

Playing Irish tunes has also been a daily reminder that our memories aren't as acute as they used to be. *Buio completo*, a complete blank, is a phrase left over from a long-ago sabbatical in Italy that comes to mind when we just can't remember how to start a tune. For me, such experiences of slippage sometimes bring a little flare of anxiety about Alzheimer's. But if we calmly go over the phrases of a tune we *do* still recall, we can eventually bring back not only the whole piece in question but also the rest of the tune-trove we've collected together over the past several years. Calmness and patience are the keys, just as I also needed to bear in mind while awaiting my six-key mopane flute. (This does leave me wondering, though, what those *other* four keys are for.) Musicians, like athletes, have the experience of getting in the zone—that state in which physical focus, tone, and the overall shape of a tune come into balance. Alertness and relaxation are both essential here. As soon as you get flustered it's time to take a walk. (Or perhaps, if you're a professional horn-player in fear of losing your chair in the orchestra, to take a beta-blocker.)

Rita and I have recently begun to pursue a practice that is called centering prayer. It is a nonverbal form of meditation that draws both on the contemplative tradition of Rita's Catholic heritage and on the Zen and Mindfulness training that has long been important to me. Not only does shared silence complement our musical conversation, it also helps us to avoid, or escape from, disabling agitation. To remember that it's counterproductive to grip our instruments or our lives too rigidly. That music, like other forms of contemplation, flows from a clear awareness of breath and heart, and manifests the body's grace.

At the heart of the pastoral tradition in literature is a dynamic (borrowing Wordsworth's terms from "Tintern Abbey") of loss and recompense. At the beginning of Virgil's first eclogue a rural neighborhood is uprooted by distant practitioners of *realpolitik* who care nothing about the small-holders being sent into exile. In such a context Tityrus's initial posture of *otium* is hardly an appropriate response, for him or for anyone else. But it does at least get something started. The conversation it provokes with the departing Meliboeus in turn prompts an authentic act of compassion and hospitality there at the shadowed edge. A modest meal and a night of shelter under a thatched roof are small things that nevertheless offer consolation. Like Lily's memories of Mrs. Ramsay as, at the table, on a porch, on the beach, she managed to bring time to a standstill and make of the moment something that endures. Like my father's impulse to offer comfort and wisdom even when he was down to only a couple of words and a scramble of letters.

The silken windings on the flute's tenons hold the instrument's three sections together and stabilize its tone. This image of adjustment and integration brings to mind two works of literature that illuminate the connections between music, marriage, and illness at this stage of our life. One of these, reaching even farther back in time than Virgil, though not quite as far as the Psalms, is the *Odyssey*. At the epic's end, when Odysseus finally makes his way home to Ithaca past Circe and Cyclops, Scylla and Carybdis, he enters a house aching from a virus of suitors. After stringing his great bronze bow the godlike hero takes them all out like a fierce dose of Prednisone. But in thinking of Rita, my own Penelope, I especially remember how Odysseus's Penelope held off that rabble of swaggering oafs so calmly and elegantly for years. Here's how Fitzgerald translates the passage from Book Nineteen in which Penelope tells her husband how she managed this.

Ruses served my turn
to draw the time out—first a close-grained web
I had the happy thought to set up weaving
on my big loom in the hall. I said, that day:
'Young men—my suitors, now my lord is dead,
let me finish my weaving before I marry,
or else my thread will have been spun in vain.
. . . .
So every day I wove on the great loom,
but every night by torchlight I unwove it;
and so for three years I deceived the Akhaians.

Weaving and unweaving, winding and unwinding, day-light, torchlight, and also our own domestic candlelight. Such rhythms hold open the possibility for music and mutual rec-ognition amid the ever-present realities of remote gods and godless invaders.

Penelope's calm, strategic flexibility makes me think not only of the unwinding and rewinding of my flute with thread spooled from an olivewood bobbin but also of Rita's clarity of spirit. As we settle into this emphatically matrimonial chapter, Rita and I are no more likely to find suitors besieging our home than we were earlier apt to find monsters or gods looming up in the hallways and classrooms of our vocational worlds. But in our comfortable old house in its quiet New England village, ill-ness has nonetheless taken up residence. Though not yet a very boisterous presence, it continually finds ways to get our atten-tion these days, like an uninvited guest who always turns the light on downstairs or makes the porch swing knock against the clapboards after we have gone to bed.

One recent evening Rita and I went for our usual after-dinner walk with Shadow. We have reconciled ourselves to the fact that hiking in the mountains will no longer be in the cards for us, and are content now to walk more sedately on the sidewalks and dirt roads of Bristol. But on this particular walk Rita discovered for the first time that it was occasionally difficult coordinating her gait even under what we had con-sidered undemanding circumstances. This new information made me want to howl. Her response, though, was a quiet and resolute one. We would just need to walk a little slower, she said, and she would want to hold onto my arm. Back in the days when her teaching and mine were at their most intense, and when our three children were all teenagers, I always thought of Rita's remarkable composure when reading Frost's poem that begins :

She is as in a field a silken tent
At midday when a sunny summer breeze
Has dried the dew and all its ropes relent,
So that in guys it gently sways at ease.

Now, as she sways in the gusts of physical change and grace-fully adjusts to the effects of rain and sun on the durable silk of her character Rita represents even more dramatically for me Frost's single-sentence paragon of a sonnet.

Through writing this book I've explored how Irish music can both give me fresh ears for pastoral poetry and offer an important resource in the face of anticipated medical challenges. But within the landscape of music, literature, and illness, the themes of marriage and memory have also come out of their cases to play together, like a concertina and a flute. Irish tunes have long had a prominent place in the music played at Vermont contra dances. And now, playing them together in our living room, I can imagine marriage and memory as a couple linking arms to promenade between other paired associations, nodding to these neighbors as they pass. Rita's and my music *is* our marriage now. Its meaning is distilled each evening as we concentrate on learning and remembering tunes that have caught our fancy. It continues to reverberate for us as we retire to the sofa after breakfast, as we debrief on last night's music or on recent books or movies we have shared, plan for the events of the day to come, laugh about the antics of our grandsons, and cast our minds back to more distant adventures, losses, and narrow escapes that have brought us to this moment and this place.

↫ "The Trip to Birmingham," with which this book's first chapter and my serious study of the flute both began, also turns out to have been one of the most challenging tunes discussed in this book. Closer to the end here they seem to have been getting simpler and simpler. I don't think it's only that I'm getting tired! Rather, just as this reflection on winding and unwinding has distilled the story to marriage and memory, so too the tunes that have been my vehicles have been simplified into melodies that rise and fall, rhythms that repeat with slight variations. These pieces, played at moderate tempo, are the ones Rita and I come back from sessions wanting to make our own. We go over them many times together, surrendering ourselves to them in a relaxed way that at the same time allows endless at-home improvisations to emerge, including harmonies, counterpoint, and rhythmic backgrounds to each other's little melodic flights. As our dear friend Jeff Hunter likes to call out at moments of domestic freedom and celebration, "Liberty Hall!"

Many of these recent favorites have been hornpipes like "The Peacock's Feather" that pulse along in fairly self-contained units of two measures. The initial two-measure unit starts on A, tumbles down through a triplet to D at the bottom of the flute's range then bounces back up to the initial A. It's such a unfraught musical foray and return, like an expansive gesture with one arm during a relaxed conversation on a warm summer morning. I'm flooded with happiness when playing it, just as I always was when hearing Rita's opening chords on the piano during her rehearsals of Beethoven's Arch-Duke Trio in Rachel's babyhood. Here's what "The Peacock's Feather" sounds like.

LINK: *The Peacock's Feather*

Not only do Beethoven's trio and this simple hornpipe both begin by sinking then immediately rising again, but they also both proceed in pairs of notes that sketch out simple thirds. This is most pronounced in the jig's second unit of two measures, which are dominated by a series of syncopated thirds, alternating between rising and falling before settling peacefully on the tonic note of a low E. The graceful opening swoop of "The Peacock's Feather," like the memory of those chords on the piano so many years ago, feels like morning air gusting through an opened window, like the sun illuminating the blowing curtain. Like a long relaxed breath allowing the pulse to slow.

It's hard with words to convey what music can mean. The fact is, this simple Irish tune recalls the sense of security I felt over sixty years ago when saying over the 23rd Psalm with my mother Lois. As babies our twin grandsons Leo and Dylan were already as sweet as could be, but their facial expressions and ways of holding their arms as they got to be several months old were also already notably different. One's alert gaze seemed to ask, "Is everything okay?" while the other's facial expression said, "I know you love me." We realized that each of them was onto something important! There are many reasons to remain watchful in this old world. In addition to the capacity to size up complex and ambiguous circumstances, though, an equally important resource for sustaining a capacity for tranquility is the impulse, at least from time, to affirm that "Surely goodness and mercy shall follow me all the days of my life." When we give ourselves to the balancing impulses of a tune like "The Peacock's Feather," then, it feels to me like gliding through the sea on my father's back. Similarly, this hornpipe's pairs of measures, each so so snugly subdivided into its own nested pairs of notes, suggests the perpetual possibility of adjustment and repair in a world that sometimes lets us in for collisions and leaves us in disarray.

When, after writing in the morning, I go downstairs to make the coffee and toast I often hear Rita in the shower repeating in a jolly voice the sentences she's worked out to bolster her verbal coordination and articulation. She has substituted drills in French and Italian for the less interesting ones her speech and language therapist originally assigned, so that she can keep up to speed on those languages at the same time. I sometimes call out when passing, "Who's in there with you anyway?" After breakfast, when I return to the study with its refreshing cross-breeze, she remains in the family room practicing what she calls her "circus arts." Standing on inflated rubber cushions that demand a constantly recalibrated sense of balance, she tosses bean bags from hand to hand. That's how it feels, too, when at the end of the day we finally settle down together in the living room to play our new favorite, "The Peacock's Feather." A simple practice of balance, repetition, and delight.

The Smuggler's Path

O'CONNELL'S TRIP
TO PARLIAMENT

In September of 2013 rita and i took our third trip to Ireland together. Its timing was determined by a couple of events we would be attending, one of them a conference at the National University of Ireland at Galway and the other a more informal gathering in Connemara. The western half of County Galway and the nearby area of Clare that includes the Burren were the parts of Ireland we had gotten to know best—a region where we'd made friends we were always eager to see as well as the setting for much of the present book. Before heading back to Galway this time around, though, we had the opportunity to spend a week and a half at another Irish friend's cottage in Kerry, a county we had never yet seen. The poet Greg Delanty, who teaches at St. Michael's College in Vermont, had offered to let us use this house near the coastal village of Derrynane. We jumped at the chance.

Perhaps jumped is too strong a word. Trekking poles turned out to be the emblems of our stay in Derrynane. Since that bout of polymyalgia several years ago I use them to buffer my knees when hiking, and now that Rita's sense of balance has been challenged by SCA she needs them too. But the poles also came to symbolize this interlude because of the fact that we nevertheless did so *much* walking there. The cottage where we were staying was just steps from the Kerry Way. From late morning until mid-afternoon on most days we pegged along that lovely path—whether heading over to the village to pick up a few supplies and enjoy a bowl of chowder at the Blind Piper, exploring the always-changing world of grass, wind, and waterfowl at the estuary in Derrynane National Park, or investigating the intricate shoreline immediately to the Park's north. Our longest foray up the coast from Derrynane followed a broken line on the little hand-drawn map run off locally for tourists. It marked a route, running parallel to the main Kerry Way, that was called the Mass Trail.

Ireland, like our home landscape in Vermont, is studded with the enormous, solitary boulders called glacial erratics. They reside where relinquished at the retreating edge of a mile-thick wedge of ice twelve thousand years ago, offering their understated commentary on the eddies and ripples of our own little agendas. During the Penal Times of the seventeenth and early eighteenth centuries, when first Cromwell and then the British Parliament and Crown attempted to suppress Irish Catholicism, priests often celebrated mass out of doors at certain erratics. As a rule the stones they chose were relatively flat on top and of altar-height, and of course located in secluded settings. Not until the Emancipation Act of 1829, inspired by Daniel O'Connell's fiery eloquence, did Ireland's Catholic majority become more fully enfranchised, not just religiously, but also in the political, economic, and educational realms.. O'Connell, known to this day as the Liberator, once lived in Derrynane House, a grand edifice that is the focal point of the National Park. Starting from there he rode toward Cork on a track called the Butter Road, then voyaged on to Westminster and Parliament.

Because our own sense of connection with Ireland is inseparable from its traditional music, the countryside is often mapped for us by the names of songs. So when we walked out from our hillside cottage in Kerry, as often as not, one of us would be absentmindedly humming or whistling the downward swoop of melody with which a favorite reel called "O'Connell's Trip to Parliament" begins.

LINK: *O'Connell's Trip to Parliament* On a spongy peninsula within the estuary we found the boulder anchoring one end of the Mass Trail and giving it its name. Though this massive gray monument was pinpointed on the map and also gestured toward by a placard at the public parking lot, it was footnoted by no sign here where it stood. This was where we started out on what ended up being an eleven-mile roundtrip from our cottage to the pier at Béaltrá. After arriving at that pier the Mass Path would turn uphill and converge with the Kerry Way, allowing us to return to Derrynane along a more level route tucked snugly into the slope between the sea and the paved highway above with its carousel of sightseeing buses. This was a considerably longer walk than we had lately been used to at home. Still, what with our trekking poles and the cheese, fruit, and cider in our backpacks—as well as lots of stops to snack, reconnoiter, tell each other what tunes were in our minds, and deliver our reports about what we had each been noticing—Rita and I completed the circuit without much fatigue. Following such a deliberate pace between the distant flicker of whitecaps and the slower pulse of boulders beside the trail, however, we did find ourselves sinking deeper and deeper into the sedimentary dream of that long-settled place.

We felt the day's confluence between past and present, Ireland and Vermont, most powerfully after our initial northward path descended all the way to the water at an unnamed (for us at least) cove. At high tide this portion of the trail would have been impassable. Even now, with the mud flats exposed, a forbidding, rocky headland rose directly before us. We searched it apprehensively for footholds, cables, or other indications of how we might make our way forward. It began to seem likely that we would have to turn back, trekking poles and all. Then we glimpsed what might have been a viable trail around to it, on a grassy hill rising more gently to our right. I ventured up first, to make sure this apparent track really went somewhere, then called back to Rita that it looked okay. We were soon atop the hill, our hearts beating from relief as well as from the climb, and gazing out to sea over the forbidding headland we had just circumvented. From this vantage point we could finally spot the cove at Béaltrá that was our goal.

After catching our breaths we continued downward on the path and soon found ourselves in a little forested bowl.

Through this copse of hazel and thorn undulated slender branches of shade-grown rowans, as sinuous and beautiful as the live oaks of my northern California boyhood. Leaning against a rock in that place of quiet beauty was a lean old gent (which is to say, a man of about my age) with a spaniel pup furiously chewing sticks at his boots. Wearing a rough brown sweater and corduroy slacks but with no cap on his tousled gray hair, he had apparently just finished his lunch and was folding a paper bag into his pocket as we came upon him in this quiet nook. He seemed in no hurry to move on, though, and quizzed us in a friendly fashion about where we had started from that day.

When we told him we had walked over on the Mass Trail from Derrynane, he replied with drawling amusement, "Well you know, I *grew up* here, and what *we* all call it is the *Smuggler's Path*." He went on to tell us that on moonlit nights in the late eighteenth and early nineteenth centuries, a number of locals—including Daniel O'Connell's uncle, from whom he inherited that impressive house in the National Park—had enriched themselves by slipping inland along this narrow track with casks of Spanish brandy destined for England. It seemed that more than one congregation had converged at the windswept rock from which we had begun.

Though our informant had no trekking poles, he was carrying a wooden staff. Eventually he hoisted himself back to his feet with it and walked on in the direction from which we had just come, just as the track of our story now continued deeper into his. The meaning of the sandy soil under our feet was changed for us by what we had heard.

As we forged on toward Béaltrá, along what we now thought of as being simultaneously the Mass Trail and the Smuggler's Path, I found myself thinking about the mysterious collision between melodies in Charles Ives's piece "General Putnam's Camp." During his boyhood in Danbury, Connecticut, Ives had listened with excitement as his bandmaster father George sent two bands marching toward each other across the common playing different pieces. Father and son both relished the resulting cacophony. It helped them discover unsuspected harmonies and sometimes even had the effect of generating entirely new melodies. Decades later, in his career as a composer, Charles wrote a number of pieces that echoed those occasions. Their sheer difficulty to play, to hear, and also to conduct (since at certain points it was necessary to beat time in three with one hand and in four with the other) seems to have delighted him.

⇌ My perspective on Ireland and its music, as well as on our home in the Green Mountains, has often been transformed like this by a stranger's casual comment, a rocky path that feels strangely familiar, or a scrap of melody that keeps returning to mind in new contexts. Such unforeseen connections have germinated in the oddly fertile soil of my scanty knowledge and clueless exhilaration, as well as in the deeper ground of teaching and family life. The startling association of a Kerry path with Ives's music was reinforced for me when we arrived in Connemara a week after the walk to Béaltrá.

We had been invited to participate in a day of conversation

organized by Tim and Máiréad Robinson in their Roundstone living room. The first person to tell her story and describe her current projects was the ecologist Micheline Sheehy Skeffington. Though her family name was new to Rita and me, it is a familiar one in modern Irish history because of her grandparents' importance to the cause of women's suffrage, the struggle for national independence, and the anti-war movement. As compelling as Micheline's tales of them were, however, our recent walk led me to be especially fascinated by her current botanical research along a variety of smugglers' paths in western Ireland.

We were all seated cozily with our mugs of tea beside a wall of windows overlooking Roundstone Bay. Micheline's jeans and windbreaker, along with her ruddy cheeks and windblown hair, reflected the fact that she and her partner Nick had just come from doing fieldwork along that gusty shore. In fact, they needed to head back out for just a few more observations after she had finished telling us about her current project and explaining why it might prove disturbing to some of the same Irish patriots who so admired the efforts of her grandparents. The briskness with which she laid out her work conveyed a scientist's long habit of distilling observations into data by which hypotheses might be tested:

> England, Scotland, and Wales have half as many species of native plants as continental Europe. That's the fate of even large islands. Ireland has fewer than half as many native plants as England. Since it is a smaller island and located farther than Britain is from the mainland that's also what one would expect. Given such a pattern, the

more purist among Irish botanists have gloried in a group
of heath-species utterly unknown in the rest of the British
Isles. These are among the plants we call 'the Irish Flora.'

Micheline went on to tell us, though, that she had concluded these members of the heather family were most likely
introduced species rather than being native to Ireland. She had
traced them back to Spain, where the same tough, spriggy plants
grow to this day and where, in the nineteenth century, they were
probably used to cushion all those small casks of brandy from
the rigors of their North Atlantic passage. I was reminded of
the cattle fodder, swept out of the holds of seventeenth-century
ships coming to New England, that introduced so many of the
European daisies, asters, chicory, and other composite species
now flourishing along the edges of our highways in Vermont.
So too this Spanish heather, dislodged from casks as they were
carried inland on smugglers' shoulders, had altered the botanical balance along either side of those night-time trails.

Although Micheline had been doing much of her work in
Galway and Donegal, recent finds in Mayo and Kerry had stimulated her interest in those areas as well. So when I told Nick
and her of the smuggler's path we had just learned about near
Derrynane they said they would definitely check it out for themselves—especially since it was near another location they had
just begun studying. Heaths cross-pollinate, so that a variety of
hybrids have now arisen beside such routes. An important part
of her research is thus to infer from today's species and hybrids
the original identity and location of the Spanish heaths from
which they derived. Even when the original plants and their

first descendants have disappeared, their genetic contributions persist within a dynamic continuum. Given that fact, it strikes me that the Irish Flora may be a good name after all for the tiny flowers that clothe these heathery slopes.

In other contexts as well, an ongoing process of transformation seems essential to the character of Ireland and its people. Just as the many Irish families who immigrated to Vermont put down their roots and grew into something new here, so too the ones who stayed home have been changed by influxes from other shores. The magnificent National Museum of Ireland in Dublin conveys an appreciation for this less essentialist view, in the prominence it gives to the history, and the elegant ships, of the Vikings. They arrived as terrifying marauders but in many cases remained to found the first Irish cities, including Dublin itself. Their story thus became inseparable from the history of Ireland. In claiming it so forcefully the museum seems to have taken the hint from Leopold Bloom in *Ulysses*, when he was challenged by the xenophobic "Citizen" to tell him what a nation was. Bloom's answer was "a group of people living in the same place at the same time."

In Derrynane we arose early each morning so that we could play a handful of our favorite tunes before setting out on the new day's walk. Among the ones we fancied then were a set of beautiful, melancholy jigs called "The One that was Lost" and "The Sheep in the Boat" that we enjoyed taking at a leisurely tempo, Vincent Broderick's wild tune "The Rookery," and, of course, "O'Connell's Trip to Parliament," which was paired with another reel called "The Torn Jacket." The fog was often rolling in as we returned from our walks in the afternoons. So

I would construct a little pyramid of turfs and kindle a fire in the fireplace. Rita took her concertina back out of its case and I reassembled my flute as a chocolaty fragrance seeped into the cottage from the glowing peat. Like those earthy blocks bearded with grass, the tunes filling the cottage every evening warmed us after another long day in the wind.

Since those idyllic days in Kerry, I have often found myself thinking back to the hybrid flora along the Smuggler's Path. There's a quality of antic proliferation both within the encompassing process of evolution and in the ceaseless ecological accommodations of a particular natural environment. Similarly, with each new step I take into traditional Irish music my sense of its intricacy grows. Like the Irish Flora, this surge of tunes manifests both a striking divergence of regional styles and a ceaseless reworking of tunes from elsewhere. The fiddler Rob Ryan suggests, for instance, that the polkas and slides of Sliebh Luachra and West Limerick were strongly influenced by the military bands—and the public dances at which they played—of Scottish regiments stationed in that contested area during the same period when traffic on the Smuggler's Path was heaviest. Many of my ideas about Irish music have similarly continued to shift with each new foray into this landscape where hybridized heaths flourish beside bogs and turfs continue to be cut.

✑ In October of 2014 I took my most recent trip to Ireland, this time without Rita's companionship. She and I were by then living in the home of our Bristol friends Jay and Joan

McEvoy as we waited for our own new, more accessible house to be completed on Mountain Street. Two more programs had been planned to honor Tim Robinson, as the final volume of his *Connemara* trilogy appeared, and I was eager to participate in them. The Royal Irish Academy was bringing out its own celebratory volume called *Connemara and Elsewhere*, which included a portfolio of Connemara images by the French photographer Nicolas Fève, several new pieces by Robinson himself related to non-Irish landscapes, and an essay by me. Presentations at the headquarters of the Academy in Dublin and at the university in Galway marked this book's launch, while an archive of Tim's manuscripts and maps was also being formally inaugurated in Galway.

Given the many decisions still required by the construction project back in Bristol, I felt that a week was the most I could devote to this trip. Still, once I got over to Ireland there turned out to be a couple of free days between scheduled events when I could pay a visit to friends living in the town of Kinvara. A chat during that pleasant interval ended up reinforcing the historical and musical collisions into which Rita and I had stumbled on the Smuggler's Path as well as coloring my perspective on all the tunes and trips that had enriched the previous four years of our life.

Kinvara is a beautiful village on the southern side of Galway Bay and thus also located near the ancient castle of DunGuaire. I had met Cilian Roden and Sabine Springer through Moya Cannon. He's a marine biologist working in both academia and commercial consultancy while she is an artist, originally from Germany, whose work reflects her professional training as a biologist. Kinvara has always reminded Rita and me of Bristol, because of both its lovely setting and the vibrant culture fostered by its mixture of families who have been there for many generations and a sizable contingent of newcomers. In Vermont such recent arrivals are called Flatlanders, while in rural Ireland the more maritime (or perhaps more botanical) term for them is Blow-ins. No one in either place seems to be in danger of forgetting who's in which category. A well known joke has a Flatlander asking a deeply rooted local if the fact that his children were born in Vermont makes them Vermonters. The response is, "If your cat has kittens in the oven does that make them biscuits?"

The fact remains, though, that both Bristol and Kinvara now have many inhabitants who, while coming from elsewhere, became integrated into their present communities decades ago. In both towns, too, there is a strong feeling of cultural richness that seems to derive in part from such diversity. One of the pubs in Kinvara has a weekly Irish session drawing people from many miles around. But on other nights it may feature American roots music and Bluegrass. At the Walkover Gallery in Bristol or up the hill at Burnham Hall in Lincoln we frequently hear the same mix of Celtic and Appalachian traditions. While our logging economy and their maritime tradition are obviously quite different, the two towns nonetheless share an attractive blend of farming, handicrafts, arts, and web-based livelihoods. In effect, there's a conversation underway in Kinvara and Bristol alike about where the vitality of rural culture will lie in this new century. In the case of Kinvara, this relates as well to the broader question of what it will mean to be Irish going forward. As a person with no Irish heritage who is nonetheless powerfully attracted to the music, literature, and landscape of Ireland, I am intrigued by Kinvara's lively example.

Cilian comes from a family that, like Micheline's, played a prominent part in the past two centuries of struggle for an independent Ireland. He is intensely interested in this history and, egged on by me, frequently talked about various aspects of it during my stay with Sabine and him. At one point, while processing something Cilian had just said, I referred to his family's role in the formation of the Irish nation. "The Irish *state*," was his reply. Since he did not elaborate upon this distinction, I inferred it was my assignment to figure out its meaning for myself.

Perhaps, I thought, it was related both to Bloom's conversation with the self-styled "Citizen" and to the emphatic inclusion of Vikings in the National Museum of Ireland. A resistance to racial essentialism, in other words. The battle for independence, Cilian might thus have been implying, was not for the purpose of establishing an ethnically based, exclusive, or chauvinistic Ireland. Rather, it aimed to set up a truly democratic state in which all citizens were fully enfranchised and responsible. In Ireland, as in America, democracy remains a work in process. The great Vermont Justice Learned Hand used to identify himself as "a citizen of the Invisible Republic." In other words, he was dedicated to beautiful ideals that had yet to be fully achieved.

A couple of months after that memorable conversation with Cilian I was back in Vermont again, playing some tunes in

John Murray's kitchen in Burlington. John has an electrifying way of playing the tenor banjo, spinning off triplets like the ones fiddlers use to elevate the intensity of reels and jigs. (Such a style is especially appropriate for a man who, following his immigration to Vermont, has established himself successfully as an electrician here.) John also shares Cilian's strong interest in modern Irish history and politics, and frequently raises related topics in conversation. So at one point in the evening, as his three large old dogs were snoozing on our stockinged feet, I told him about Cilian's distinction between a nation and a state. John pondered this for a moment over his cup of tea and then looked up to declare, "But there *is* also an Irish nation, you know." Catching my breath after the solemn way in which he stated this, I asked, "What is it, then?" "The Irish nation," John said, "is everyone all around the world who loves playing Irish music."

These linked conversations with Cilian and John reverberate with the stimulating affinities I have discovered between Ireland and Vermont. They also speak to the ways in which playing Irish music continues to influence my relationships with neighbors in Bristol and to Rita's and my ongoing attempts to shape a chapter of our marriage that feels sometimes like an elegy but more often like a surprise party.

Sky over the Common

THE BATTERING RAM
AND LUCY FARR
~

As the summer of 2014 approached, and right after the surprisingly quick sale of our house on North Street, Rita and I drove up to Craftsbury to get it the cabin ready for the new season. Once the weather has gotten warmer we enjoy coming up for visits of several days to a week from our home in Bristol—about two hours to the south. On this particular stay, after mud season had come and (finally) gone, we scythed the dandelion-spangled grass around the cabin, brushed the cobwebs off the screens, followed disconcerting puffs of stench to a dead mouse in our loft, and scrubbed out the wood-fired hot tub in preparation for a season of soaking. Unlike when Nicholas Williams came by before Christmas and taught me "The Month of January," the days were extravagantly long now. After eight in the evening the shining surface of Little Hosmer Pond was dominated by a sharply focused, if inverted, reflection of the cedar trees crowding the eastern shore. A smaller portion of the pond, beside the screened porch where Rita and

I sat in our rockers after dinner, still mirrored the cloudy sky. With all those shadow cedars pointing their spires so sharply into the pond, the twilight seemed to be both rippling around our dock and hanging above it. We too, rocking on that porch, felt ourselves floating upward and at the same time sinking downward. This sense of vertigo was enhanced by the loons calling to each other from the far northern shore of Little Hosmer Pond. Roberta Alexander, a neighbor to our south on the pond who sold us the land for this cabin twenty years ago, always referred to that thicket of reeds and water lilies from which disembodied loon calls now issued as the Stephen King Corner. *Oh-OOOooo. Oh-OOOooo.* At midnight we would awaken to their wilder ululations from much closer at hand, urgent bulletins from a world in which owls and snapping turtles were cruising uncomfortably close to their newly laid eggs.

Come daytime, the loons were generally silent, solemnly paddling around the pond as a self-possessed couple then suddenly disappearing—*Bloop! Bloop!*—when one of them dove into a school of little yellow perch passing just below them and the mate almost immediately swept down for a snack too. There was also a much rowdier couple of Canada geese working the waters of Little Hosmer. They flew up and down its length ceaselessly and very low, wingtips sometimes patting the pond as they honked mightily. We suggested to our Australian shepherd Shadow, who's black and white like those large birds, that they were barking at her and she might want to give them a piece of her mind. But she knew the difference between a goose and a dog and regarded them with equanimity from her patch of recently scythed grass near the dock.

Such a perfectly coordinated flight by this pair of geese, even amid that honking hubbub, recalled the end of Frost's lovely poem of marriage, "The Master Speed." He introduces his double-metaphor of rowing and flying with these lines: "No speed of wind or water rushing by/But you have speed far greater." And he concludes it, ". . . life is only life forevermore/ Together wing to to wing and oar to oar." Frost wrote this poem for the wedding of his daughter Irma, a troubled offspring of that psychologically fragile family. What he had seen of the new couple had left him fearful about their future, and indeed it wasn't long before Irma left her husband. It's all the more moving, then, to find the poet and father attempting to graft into that new marriage the beautiful unity he had observed in a pair of birds amid the saturated beauty of June in northern New England.

So often we glimpse the truth of our own emotional lives in those of birds and animals, or at any rate look for it there. While watching these couples of loons and geese, mated like us for life, Rita and I can't help seeing a reflection in the pond of our time in the cabin beside it. What they're really saying when they call we can no more make out than Shadow can. Still, their passionately affiliated existence near at hand makes them stirring neighbors for us. This is our place to come as a couple now, after the drama and the comedy of child-rearing. Though we enjoy referring to the cabin as our honeymoon cottage, we do not forget that we are concluding our life together rather than just beginning it. We come here to dive like those loons, like those inverted cedars, into a shimmering pond of memory.

Meanwhile, though, a more raucous message was rattling our elegiac windows. At five o'clock every morning a handsome young sapsucker stationed himself on the metal insert at the top of our cabin's brick chimney. We had installed this cap a few winters back, after we arrived one weekend for some cross-country skiing only to find that a plug of ice in the chimney made it impossible for us to have a fire in the stove of our frigid cabin. We had to seek shelter with Russell and Janet Spring, our only year-round neighbors on the western side of Little Hosmer. The sapsucker in question now perched on the base of this insert, right below the overhanging cap, and set to work telegraphing the song of himself to the neighborhood.

An ornithologist friend once told us that most birdcalls essentially translate to "I'm over here!" This of course implies different things at different moments of the year. At some seasons it might mean "My nest! Stay away!" At other less fraught times it might simply celebrate a sense of well-being: "It's a grand day to perch just here and nowhere else!" But after each burst of this sapsucker's rhythmic self-expression, amplified by that crowning circle of sheet metal as crisply as Souza marches bounce off the artfully angled ceiling of a New England bandstand, he noticeably cocked his head to listen for a reply. His tense eagerness for an acknowledgement suggested that this particular message was more like "Love! Over here! Hurry!" He would peck away for a half an hour during his first visit of the morning, rousing us from our warm bed to make coffee, wrap ourselves in blankets, sit on the porch, and watch the lingering mist swirl over the pond. But he would also return at intervals over the next twelve hours. Pecking, listening, waiting, departing, returning, pecking some more. Though he was unsuccessful at attracting companionship during the several days of our visit, this little bird with the natty black-and-white plumage on his breast remained undaunted.

As we listened to him with sympathetic, if increasingly exhausted, interest, I heard in his characteristic opening riff the same rhythm with which "Langstrom Pony" begins: Rat-a-TAT-TAT, TAT-TAT-ta-TAT-TAT-ta-TAT-TAT-ta. Subsequent pecking by the sapsucker during visits to the chimney cap never remained so predictable and regular. But because "Langstrom Pony" itself is so consistent in its narrow rhythmic and harmonic range, once the bird had suggested this musical association the whole tune began to run through my mind whenever that tapping on our chimney cap commenced. The jig also became code for "sapsucker" in this early-summer sojourn at the camp. Such an automatic association reminded me of when I was enrolled in first-year Japanese at Middlebury College, working so hard at vocabulary and dialogues, often way past midnight, that when I would slip into bed beside Rita and close my eyes certain words and phrases would burst into my hearing as if spoken aloud. I had simply pressed too much Japanese into my brain for it to be contained there for very long.

During that period Rita and I took a weekend holiday in Montréal and headed to dinner at a Pyrenean restaurant we had heard great things about. Her command of French is beautiful and mine is adequate, so we felt relaxed about our various exchanges with the rather formal but solicitous waiter. After we had settled into our meal (a memorable cassoulet for me) he came up to ask if we liked it. We were of course conversing in English at the time, and as I flicked the foreign-language switch in my brain Japanese brusquely shouldered French aside so that instead of responding "oui" I almost shouted with enthusiasm, "Hai!" Rita, he, and I were equally nonplussed by this moment. Where did *that* come from? The answer seemed to be that, after weeks of intense repetition, certain words and phrases had staked out their claim to the front of my linguistic queue.

Learning Irish tunes by ear has made both Rita and me much more aware of such vagaries of memory. It can take a while for us to feel entirely secure in a new tune. Even when it's relatively simple there will be some surprising sequence of notes or a variation (Benedict's "forks in the road") in what might have seemed initially just the repetition of an earlier section. We have gotten better at taking tunes in aurally, and often have almost memorized a tune the other one has been working on simply by hearing him or her play it over and over around the house. Still, when one of us wants to learn such an overheard tune more confidently, and asks the other one to play it more slowly line by line, pausing over tricky details, there's invariably some painstaking work to be done. Recently Rita asked me to help her iron out "The Battering Ram" in this way. Because this three-part jig had been one of the tunes introduced in Hilari and Benedict's workshop on Clare repertoire that I took but she did not, it had been one of those much-heard pieces around our house. In going over it together now we experienced an increasingly familiar phenomenon related to our process of memorization. Namely, that while we no longer feel much need to see the music written out while learning a tune we do often find it helpful to *describe*, to each other, and to ourselves, what happens in certain tricky parts.

One detail of the tune that she was stumbling over turned out to be at a place I was not really in control of either, so we both went back to the CD I had been given at the conclusion of the workshop. The question was whether one three-note grouping in the A section went up and down and up again, B-A-B, or just went down, B-A-G. The answer turned out to be the latter, and though either choice would have worked within the basic harmony of the jig, hitting the G was definitely more effective musically. Especially as we began to get "The Battering Ram" up to speed we could hear that the tune swung back and forth between strongly played D's and G's, establishing a bright fifth as the interval at its heart. I have the impression that one characteristic of Irish music might be a preference for fifths over thirds in its underlying harmonic structures. Be that as it may, getting a detail like this right can intensify a tune's flavor. Here goes.

LINK: *The Battering Ram*

Even though, for us aging newcomers to Irish music, it may sometimes be helpful to talk through perplexing aspects of a tune like this, though, the subsequent process of repeating it dozens of times is what really consolidates our sense not just of its notes but also of its defining patterns and decisive moments. In other words, the tune itself teaches us how to find the *music* within it. Even when we're playing certain tunes together, however, there is also another level of learning that becomes ever more specific to our particular instruments: muscle memory.

Tunes that are up to speed no longer allow for naming the notes. Rather, your fingers must learn on their own where to jump and when, as if they had a mind of their own. The fingers' muscle memory *activates*, just as it is activated *by*, the brain. This phenomenon relates as well to one of the mysterious satisfactions of playing with others after having learned hundreds of tunes by ear. If asked about a given tune you might well come up blank. But when another player launches into it as you sit there with your own instrument the whole piece is suddenly there for you and you're playing along without a care.

The mysterious and satisfying interaction of mind and fingers, within that collective exercise of memory known as an Irish session, can have the same organic unfolding as a conversation. Wholeness emerges as friends come together, having done nothing by way of planning, to weave a new fabric from disparate memories, insights, imagery, and feelings. Since marriage is my chief context for both these modes of shared experience, I relate such confluence to the description in the wedding ceremony of two people becoming "one flesh." And also, in our own case, to the transformation of two autonomous individuals into "parents"—those who share.

Our recent exploration of centering prayer has fed my interest in ancient monastic traditions. In this context I have recently been reading Kathleen Norris's book *The Cloister Walk*, in which she describes her experiences as a Benedictine oblate. Much of her focus is on the prominence of the Psalms in the monastery's daily practice. "To say or sing the psalms aloud within a community," she writes, "is to recover religion as an oral tradition, restoring to our mouths words that have been snatched from our tongues and relegated to the page, words that have been privatized and effectively silenced. It counters our tendency to see individual experience as sufficient for for-mulating a vision of the world." For Rita and me, the aural and collective transmission of Irish music too is a lifting up of our individuality into a larger, shared awareness. Marriage and lit-erature may resemble such music to the extent that they too encourage us to make ourselves at home in a world encom-passing but not restricted to our little selves.

↜ Memorizing, then continually revisiting, the endless, modal permutations of so many tunes means that one or another of them is almost always in my head. Just as I couldn't help recalling "Langstrom Pony" when listening to the sapsucker's tapping, so too I often slip into a wild reel like "Swinging on a Gate" when pedaling my ancient three-speed bike Rocinante as fast as I can go down North Street on a brisk May morning. Or without thinking about it I adjust my breathing, and even my pulse, to the lazy arcs of a favorite slip-jig like "Give Me a Drink of Water" or "A Fig for a Kiss" when I stretch out after lunch for that retiree's delight, a nap. Though these connections are not intentional, or even necessarily conscious, they can still bring unity and rhythm to otherwise mundane moments. Such *dis-covery*, rather than deliberate *formulation*, of life's meaning is particularly apt to occur now in retirement, when life is not so firmly framed by an institutional agenda. In that regard, it reflects the reality that my days now, while purposeful in their own way, are more like poking around the Hundred Aker

Wood than like heading dutifully to campus, briefcase in hand. (*Rum-tum-tiddle-um-tum.*)

Unanticipated intersections between Irish music and little daily discoveries also reverberated for me with another central element of pastoral literature. The core themes in this literary lineage include the love of nature, the enduring importance of childhood experiences, the reality of personal loss, and the recovery of wholeness through creative memory. Wordsworth relates the concept of "spots of time" to such a process of "renovation"—as noted in the Prologue to this book. When certain experiences attain the intensity of what he calls "rememberable things" a specific moment and a particular location are fused into a personal landmark. They become enduring and recoverable, unlike other experiences which may be swept away in a forgettable jumble. Similarly, a musical phrase that enters unbidden into my mind quickly prompts a recollection of the whole tune, muscle-memory, name, and all. Music and meaning pulse back enriched by overtones and harmonics, just as the notes in that descending passage of "The Battering Ram" thread a labyrinth of kindred and resonant possibilities.

Returning in this context to "spots of time" brings into focus other details from the passage in Wordsworth's *Prelude* where he explores this idea. In thinking about how certain moments from childhood return to him in adulthood and suffuse his entire vision of life, Wordsworth writes:

There are in our existence spots of time,
That with distinct pre-eminence retain
A renovating virtue, whence—depressed

By false opinion and contentious thought,
Or aught of heavier or more deadly weight,
In trivial occupations, and the round
Of ordinary intercourse—our minds
Are nourished and invisibly repaired . . .
                              . . . Such moments
Are scattered everywhere, taking their date
From our first childhood.

Now that our dedication to traditional Irish music has collided with Rita's ataxia, the meaning of this passage which I have so often discussed with students at Middlebury has deepened for me. A progressive neurological disorder could also be described as a degenerative one, if related solely to the evidence of an MRI. And the inescapability of that fact could easily become, as Wordsworth says, "depressing." But the coloring of our daily experience by shared rhythms and melodies has truly bestowed on us its "renovating virtue." Through it our hearts have been "invisibly repaired" in ways that help us bear up to this genetically encoded change in Rita's cerebellum. This is no mere literary trope. It is a vital fact of our life together for which poetry has prepared both of us.

Wordsworth aspired to be an epic poet, measuring himself especially against his literary inspiration Milton. The story that he had to tell, though, turned out to be a more surprising cluster of meanings, "scattered everywhere" in his memory but occurring especially in his "first childhood," when he first opened himself to winds sweeping across the expanses of the Lake District. Even as a boy he had forged out into nature with an intensity of expectation, glorying in his power as he both stole eggs from bird nests and stole a skiff tied up along a wooded shore. But it was the terror and remorse he ultimately experienced at such moments of intended masterfulness that dilated the apertures of his eyes, mind, and heart, imprinting such surprises indelibly in his memory.

In retirement I have stumbled into a similarly nourishing dialectic between expectation and actuality when trying to hold up my end of the bargain as Rita and I expand our repertoire of Irish tunes. At times when I am playing alone rather than with Rita, I concentrate on technical challenges like adapting my embouchure to achieve a fuller tone in the upper register (more muscle-memory needed here too) or gaining speed and fluidity when I tap with the gawky third finger of my left hand when performing an A roll. But when we subsequently are playing together we are both reminded that the music's deeper meaning has much more to do with receptivity than with technical striving and accomplishment.

Over the past decade and a half Rita and I have enjoyed visiting her many second and third cousins (with all these degrees of familial relationship snugly covered by that lovely Italian term *i parenti*). Most of them still live in the same ancient hilltown east of Rome called Artena, from which both of her maternal grandparents came. Before the first such trip she kindly collected a number of ready-made phrases to help me paddle along with my scanty Italian amid all those ebullient conversations. (A couple of glasses of wine definitely helped on such occasions too.) We still have fun using these Italian formulas back in the safe confines of our Bristol home, such as when we are playing after dinner. When it's my turn to start a new set, for instance, she'll often call out, "*Tocc' a te.*" On such occasions I don't deliberate much about what should come next, but on impulse simply break into something suggested in a conscious or unconscious way by what we were just playing. A tune just starts playing *me*, and within three notes we'll be gliding along together, wing to wing and key to key. We two, and our quite different yet both audibly breathing instruments, take in and sing out the music that's filling our room and our minds like oxygen.

The discovery that effort can eventually become a scaffolding for receptivity bears not only on our experience of music within the spacious world of retirement but also on other unforeseen opportunities of this moment in our marriage. Just as terror and confusion opened Wordsworth to the larger life of nature as a young boy so too Rita's diagnosis has deepened our relationship through a shared need for resilient inwardness. In the same way that one's mind can become more supple and receptive when emptied of distractions, so too can a tune. Concentration is of course necessary if one is to play well. But the capacity to let go of intellectual control is also essential. This is actually one of the benefits of maintaining a rock-solid rhythm in the dance forms, as I have recently discovered. One night not long ago Rita and I just kept playing "Swinging on a Gate" and "Miss McLeod's" over and over again, with other tunes occasionally interspersed just so that we could then return to those first two tunes afresh. As we emphasized the pulse, with a goal of playing absolutely together regardless of whether we were on the fast side or going a bit slowly, we also found ourselves shaping the music more deftly on the levels of dynamics, tonal variety, and phrasing. In other words, by giving ourselves up to the rhythm we gained the grace of each of these tunes' delicate musical character.

The rhythm embraces and lifts up the melody then, just as the tunes carried in our bodies and minds can help to shape the events of each day into wholeness. Shapeliness in any one part of our lives becomes a meme replicated in other aspects of experience, a beat to which we may move through widely varying forms of work and play. Which brings me back again to the alluring strangeness of Irish tunes' names. As Cieran Carson has written, they sometimes feel reminiscent of the Dada-like names of rock bands when I was growing up in the San Francisco Bay Area: Electric Flag, Jefferson Airplane, Country Joe and the Fish. But there are also some recurrent patterns among the Irish tunes' titles. In the course of writing this I've mentioned "Banish Misfortune" several times, not only as a favorite tune but also as a title that sums up for me Irish music's spirit of defiance in the face of centuries of suffering.

Yet another title, relevant specifically to the Great Hunger, is that of "The Battering Ram"—one of this chapter's leit-motifs. The name of this strongly cadenced tune refers to the horrific instruments carried by teams of landlords and officials coming to break down the doors when farmers' families were being evicted from their cottages and removed from their land. In Virgil's Lombardy and in nineteenth-century Ireland alike, such evictions were the terrible consummation of a community's destruction. Hilari told us that there are to this day musicians in Clare who won't play the tune because of these associations with its title. Nevertheless, its endurance in the tradition also conveys a determination to prevail over the oppressiveness of the past, by naming and defying rather than forgetting it. "Banish Misfortune" similarly speaks to the role of this music in consoling and healing Rita and me, in the face of medical challenges that allow for no healing apart from endurance and celebration.

Atmospheric tone-poems like "The Mist-Covered Mountain" and "Out on the Ocean" are well represented by their titles. When I speak these names I feel the same mood as when the music itself fills my heart. Topographic titles like "Lough Derg" and "Dunguaire" pinpoint spots of time on the map of our travels in Ireland. Like the Irish names that Tim Robinson has dedicated himself to helping restore, such titles of tunes have taken on personal associations for Rita and me too—with particular picnics, hikes, and conversations that were essential to our growing love for western Ireland. To hear the name, play the tune, or visit the place is to recover in each case a complex, unified, and enduring experience. One title that has become an especially charged one for me is "My Darling Asleep." It's a tune Rita and I frequently play, since it goes well in several different sets. When, in the candle-lit living room, I glance at her over the top of my flute I often see her face gazing into the middle distance with the endearingly vacant expression known as the "concertina stare." At such moments, after forty-five years of marriage, I can't help also imagining her face on the pillow as she sleeps in bed or tucked into a corner of the family-room sofa as she grabs a nap under the woolen Irish throw after supper.

Vivid personal images step forward from the titles of songs, just as the wholeness of a family's life may be evoked by a scattering of snapshots. The startling power of these associations recalls the perpetual surprise of being swept up into a tune after hearing only its first two or three notes. Listening to a hermit thrush singing around our little cedar cabin at Camp Lois prompts similarly powerful memories for us. This thrush's song, which is such an emotional and at the same time ethereal element of the northern forest, had seemed to us less and less common over the past decade. In the midst of worries about both our own physical unwinding and the impact of climate change on the forests and wildlife of Vermont we sometimes worry that the local populations of Vermont's signature songbird might be dwindling away—whether from ecological loss close at hand or because of destruction of its winter habitat in Central America.

But on each of the days on this recent visit when we were awakened by the drumming of the sapsucker on our chimney cap we ended up hearing the hermit thrush on our subsequent walks together. Whether we were forging south through the thin screen of trees between our cabin and the Springs' house so that we could pay a visit to Russell and Janet, heading over to enjoy the delicious breeze that swept across Pat's Point, just to our north, or taking a longer outing along the dirt and gravel of Wiley Hill Road, with its overarching sugar maples and its hayfields, ponds, and homesteads, we heard the hermit thrushes calling around us. We were particularly aware of thrushes singing in the cool of the morning and again as the early evening's shadows began to fall from the hill rising steeply just behind and to the west of our cabin.

Camp Lois is a place where Rita and I especially enjoy memorizing and reciting Frost's poems together. One of these that we like to shout out laughingly while swimming in the pond or pumping water into the hot tub is "Come In," with its exuberant beginning, "As I came to the edge of the woods, / Thrush music—hark!" But if the unexcelled beauty of this bird's song always makes us stop and exclaim to one another, it also has a hauntingly recessive quality. Two strong opening tones followed by a tone of transitional strength suddenly give way to delicate ripples of quieter, subtler notes that shimmer into silence. Frost evokes the always receding beauty of thrushes calling through the shadows of a New England forest in two remarkable lines later in the poem: "Far in the pillared dark / Thrush music went—" Even as we listen with all our might in the first instant of noticing it, this music is departing from us. I've lost some acuteness in my capacity to hear high frequencies over the last several years. (Perhaps from all that flute playing . . .) When on our walks Rita asks if I can hear the white-throated sparrow that routinely perches in a meadow beside Wiley Hill Road I often have to allow, regretfully, that I do not. In the case of the hermit thrushes, though, on this recent visit to the camp, I could always at least hear those strong opening tones. After that, the whispery glissando that finished the call could at least be supplied, in my memory, by echoes of other thrushes at the close of other days.

In "Tintern Abbey" Wordsworth gives thanks for "... all the mighty world/Of eye and ear,—both what they half create,/And what perceive." Memory and imagination can fill out the fragmentary status of our experience, ushering us back into the wholeness of the world. Our bodies may begin, must begin, to unwind at the genetic and cellular levels, whether through chromosomal disassembly or through the unheard breakage of cilia deep in the inner ear. Our memories may draw a blank when asked to play a tune unheard for many months. Then the past is recollected, the future re-imagined. Two notes were all I needed to hear the hermit thrushes' entire song, in my ear and in my heart. Winding the black thread from the bobbin back onto the tenon, then waxing it into the compact fragrance of the joint, I can reassemble the flute and play a tune. Clockwise goes the thread, clockwise the twisting of the blackwood joints, clockwise the untwisting when it's time to take the flute apart again and swab it out before returning it to the green velvet interior of its case. Or <u>sunwise</u>, as the Abenaki say because of the direction of the sunrise's seasonal rotation around the horizon.

As I conclude this exploration of how picking up the flute, marriage, retirement, and pastoral literature have become so interwound with each other in my life, another title of a tune that's on my mind is "Come West Along the Road." (We play it as the second part of a set with "The Maids of Mt. Kisco.") It's a melody whose most delightful element is the recurrence of quick ascending triplets throughout the B part. Though I like the tune for itself I haven't yet played it enough for it to inflect other parts of my life. So I'm struck at this point mostly by its title's simplicity and directness—suggesting one of those little "prayer sentences" Thomas Keating recommends using to sustain a receptive spirit between sessions of centering prayer. The fact that it takes the form of an invitation also reminds me of Tityrus's offer of hospitality to Meliboeus at the end of the first Eclogue. When Rita and I head out for our walk after supper we generally pause at the vantage point behind the high school so that we can gaze across at the distant glowing Adirondacks. The title of the tune comes to mind on these occasions, with its own suggestion of a westward stroll together at the end of a long, eventful day. Of a relaxed moment in which there's no need for an agenda beyond the rhythm of the walk and pleasure of companionship.

✍ Before heading back down to Bristol, Rita and I had a chance to play some tunes with a friend named Carol Dickson following a graduation-related event at Sterling College in Craftsbury. I serve on the board of this school devoted to environmental stewardship while Carol both teaches there and is Dean of the Faculty. Since she's also an excellent fiddler we had arranged to get together with her after the day's formal program was over. Most buildings on the campus were busy with other activities that evening, so we decided to play in the nineteenth-century bandstand at one end of the Common. Rita, Carol, and I accordingly reconvened there in the early-summer gloaming of northern Vermont. We could still see each other clearly as we climbed the steps of that small, elevated bandstand and took our places on the benches built around the walls. But as we played the first several sets the light became noticeably dimmer, lending a quality of muffled transparency to everything around us. The night stayed warm, though, and also harbored a delicious, intermittent breeze. Though the surrounding Common was now in darkness, yellow lights blinked on like fireflies in a few of the white clapboard buildings around its edges. In the western sky, beyond the church and library, a broad purple streak continued to glow between two low layers of gray cloud while more and more stars emerged above them.

Carol's special interest is in the music of Québec, while we have of course been devoting ourselves primarily to Irish music. Still, we never ran out of tunes we all knew well enough to play together. We started with a couple of tunes Rita and I proposed, "Out on the Ocean" and the "Carraroe Jig," then slid into a couple of Carol's favorite reels, the "Gaspé" and "St. Anne's." Back and forth we went, delighted by the interplay of these traditions, and reminded once again by their companionable accord that the Breton and Norman origin of many francophone Canadians has always aligned their music with that of other Celtic musical cultures. Another influence of course came from the fact that Montréal received a huge influx of Irish immigrants in the later nineteenth century.

At one point we began a long mixed set of waltzes, including a favorite of ours called "Louie's Waltz" that we had learned from the CD of a lively young group of Irish and Irish-American musicians calling themselves NicGaviskey and that we now taught Carol. We all already knew and loved the "Ook

Pik," or "Canada" waltz, and found ourselves playing it over and over with variations, swept along by its pulsing rhythms. Then we learned an entrancing tune called "The Haapavesi Waltz" from Carol. It was composed by a Canadian musician named Keith Murphy who presently lives in southern Vermont and was inspired by his own encounters with some traditional Finnish musicians. Rita and I played it a slowly a few times after Carol gave this waltz to us line by line, and when we were solid on it she added a lovely harmony which her fiddle teacher Becky Tracy helped her work up for this unusual melody. As we took turns with that harmony, as well as experimenting with other variations that came to mind, we felt a growing desire to inhabit each tunc for a long time as we floated together in that bowl of stars.

After we had been playing for a while a young man climbed up into the bandstand with us. We could barely make him (or each other) out by then and he settled in on an empty bench without speaking. He remained there in companionable silence for quite some time, inspiring in us a new, more vibrant sense of relationship with the lovely old village above which we were spinning out our tunes. We stopped speaking at this point too, out of a tacit desire to affirm his own stillness and attentiveness. Rather than disrupting the experience of intimacy in that elevated space, our unknown listener thus deepened it even as he introduced the exciting sense of an audience close at hand and listening carefully to every note. Eventually, at a break between sets, he said thank you and goodbye, climbing back down to earth as we sent our own goodbyes after him.

It was getting late, and we wondered whether it might be time to put our instruments back in their cases. But we found it hard to stop playing while it was still reasonably warm out and there was at least a bit of light in the sky. So we moved into a little march we all knew called "Lucy Farr." This is a remarkably simple tune, with a lot of similarity between the A and B parts. Its innate, mesmerizing repetitiveness, plus our recent experience with playing Keith Murphy's waltz so many times, led us into a long sequence of variations on this undemanding and appealing piece, sometimes playing off-beats against our companions' unison, at other points holding certain tones as a drone or discovering appealing counter-melo-

LINK:
Lucy Farr

dies to slip in and out of. Soon after we realized this would be the last tune we shared that evening we spotted several people doing a free-form dance to our music on the dark common immediately below the bandstand. We couldn't make out their faces or clothing at all, but the gleam of bare arms and legs suggested that they may have been women from the graduating class at Sterling College, clothed in light summer dresses for this evening of celebration before the next day's Commencement exercises.

There was a wonderfully spontaneous quality to the dancing below us, with the four or five of them (we couldn't tell just how many) moving in a loose circle, sometimes gathering close together then scattering suddenly apart as the music of this elementary little march pulsed along. Our dim and intermittent glimpses of the dancers' limbs made them resemble a wisp of mist hovering above a still Vermont pond in the hour after dark. A swirl of vapor holding together for a few moments, before being dispersed into thin air by a gust of wind. They danced, we played, and played some more, then finally stopped. As soon as we did that wisp of dancers too faded away over the quiet common. We called our thanks and good wishes after them but by then they were gone.

Acknowledgments

⤳

Early on in this project I was fortunate enough to meet Catherine McEvoy and Brad Hurley, two splendid flute players who became my generous teachers throughout the adventure. Along the way I also had the benefit of taking individual lessons with Chris Norman and Nicholas Williams and of participating in workshops taught by each of them and by Kevin Crawford. Forbes and Yolanta Christie, proprietors of Windward Flutes, made my prized keyless and keyed flutes as well as offered essential guidance in the care of these wooden instruments.

Jefferson Hunter, Sue Halpern, Scott Sanders, and John Tallmadge have all been kind enough to read *Picking Up the Flute* in its entirety, offering extremely discerning and helpful responses as it progressed from stage to stage. Highly illuminating advice about particular sections also came from Moya Cannon, Ray Coish, Lauret Savoy, Tom Slayton, Jennifer

Green-Lewis, Bill McKibben, Marion Wells, Victor Luftig, Elizabeth Fowler, David Brynn, and Randy Ganiban. Several chapters derive in part from pieces previously published in *Archipelago*, edited by Andrew McNeillie; *Unfolding Irish Landscapes*, edited by Christine Cusick and Derek Gladwin; *Passion*, edited by Larry Yarbrough; and *A Landscape History of New England*, edited by Richard Judd and Blake Harrison. I remain grateful to these gifted and supportive editors. I also want to express special appreciation to Liz Carroll for her permission to record "Island of Woods" for this project.

Tim Robinson's deeply grounded and far-reaching books on the Aran Islands and Connemara galvanized my understanding of the history, culture, and terrain from which Ireland's indomitable music has emerged. I also want to thank both Tim and Máiréad Robinson for hosting a series of conversations, at their home in the village of Roundstone, where I first encountered an extraordinary community of writers, scientists, artists, and conservationists from Connemara and Galway. Moya Cannon and John Roden, Nicolas Fève, Cilian Roden and Sabine Springer, Leslie Van Gelder, Jane Conroy and John Waddell, and Nessa Cronin and Dara Scott have all offered insights and companionship essential to my writing during the four-year period covered here.

Benedict Koehler and Hilari Farrington's School of Irish Traditional Music regularly sponsors workshops on repertoire and regional styles. These have been lovely resources for lovers of Irish music in central Vermont. The session at Jericho Tavern organized by Maria Wicker, Denise Dean, and Beth Jillson and the occasional gatherings at Jonathan Leonard's house in Richmond have offered valuable opportunities to play this fundamentally sociable music with kindred spirits. My wife Rita and I have also reveled in frequent opportunities to play favorite tunes with musical friends like Shel Sax, John Murray, Joyce and Ken Wolpin, Jim McGinniss and Clare Doyle, and Jim Haggerty and Jean Withrow, in their homes and in ours.

Working with Dede Cummings and her colleagues at Green Writers Press has truly been a joy. I've never found more skilled and supportive editors than Rose Alexandre-Leach and Dede herself, while the support of editor Sierra Dickey and the close reading of Ron Anahaw have also advanced the project in important ways. I greatly appreciated the contributions of Michael Chorncy at his Goose Coop studio too, as he oversaw the recording of the audio book and flutetracks with such calming expertise.

In her excellence as a reader, a traveling companion, and a musical partner, as well as in her wisdom about the meaning of retirement and the path of wholeness, my wife Rita has been the central and indispensable influence on this memoir. It is dedicated to her.

CPSIA information can be obtained at www.ICGtesting.com
Printed in the USA
LVOW07s2123161016

508873LV00006B/8/P